I 've found that you can call yourself anything," said Harris, "but it's what's going on inside that makes all the difference." He sat down on a rock, and Jayne sat beside him, marveling at how radically different this conversation was from the one she had just experienced. With Harris she felt safe and comfortable, and almost totally at ease.

Jayne smiled. "Faith is a strange thing. Sometimes I think I have it almost figured out, and then someone like Derrick comes along, professing to be this great Christian, and when things turn rotten, it blows my tiny theology to pieces. Which turned out to be a good thing in the long run—I can't believe I almost married the wrong man."

Harris leaned his head back and looked up at the stars. "So, do you think you'll know when the right one comes along?"

Jayne studied his face in the moonlight, then nodded. "I think so."

HEARTLAND SKIES

Melody Carlson

PALISADES

HEARTLAND SKIES
published by Palisades
a division of Multnomah Publishers, Inc.

© 1998 by Melody Carlson
International Standard Book Number: 1-57673-264-9

Cover illustration by Glenn Harrington
Design by Brenda McGee

Scripture quotations are from:
The Holy Bible, New International Version © 1973, 1984 by International Bible Society, used by permission of Zondervan Publishing House

Printed in the United States of America

For information:
MULTNOMAH PUBLSISHERS, INC.•POST OFFICE BOX 1720•SISTERS, OREGON 97759

Library of Congress Cataloging-in-Publication Data:
Carlson, Melody.
    Heartland skies/by Melody Carlson
        p.   cm.
    ISBN 1-57673-264-9 (paper)
    I. Title.
PS3553.A73257H43   1998
813'.54—dc21   97–36406
                                                                CIP

98 99 00 01 02 03 04 — 10 9 8 7 6 5 4 3 2 1

With special thanks to my sister and friend,
Melisa McDonald,
for her equestrian expertise
and firsthand experience in the land of cowboys.

Blessed are the peacemakers,
for they will be called sons [daughters] of God.

MATTHEW 5:9

ONE

❖

N ow, here's a serious contender for this year's all-around buckaroo award," said the rodeo announcer. "Mac Lawson, from Lubbock, Texas, already holds this year's saddle bronc record. Today he's riding Black Rage. Let's hear it, cowboys and cowgirls—put your hands together for Mac on Black!"

Jayne Morgan watched with wide eyes as the black horse sprang out of the gate, bucking and twisting. He was a good-looking horse, and he moved with agility. As silver spurs dug into his flanks, the horse spun wildly.

She winced as the fiery stallion again bucked high into the air, this time showing daylight below. The crowd exploded with wild cheering. As the horse landed, he threw down his head impossibly low, and the rider was thrown against his neck. In the next moment, both horse and rider tumbled into a bone-crushing somersault, with the cowboy landing on the bottom. Jayne gasped and covered her eyes.

The crowd grew hushed for an instant, and then a low rumble of concerned murmuring began. Jayne couldn't bring herself to look. The announcer was saying something about how these things happened in the rodeo world so the audience shouldn't be worried. The words barely registered with Jayne; her heart was pounding, and she wished she hadn't come to the rodeo.

"Is he okay?" she whispered to her fiancé, Derrick Long, her eyes still closed.

"Yep, he's fine. Just a little shook up is all. See—he's getting up and walking around. No big deal, Jayne." The crowd began to clap hesitantly, and Jayne finally opened her eyes and stared down into the arena. There in a quivering mound lay what had only moments ago been a strong and healthy horse. Two rodeo hands were examining him.

"We have experienced help available who know how to handle these situations," the announcer said in a calm voice; and then he added more quietly, "Could we please have our rodeo veterinarian report to Gate C immediately."

"I thought you said he was just fine!" Jayne grabbed Derrick by the arm.

"He is," said Derrick as he pointed down to the other end of the arena. "See, there's Mac right—"

"I meant the horse!" she hissed.

Derrick laughed. "You mean you were more worried about the horse than the cowboy? Mac took quite a fall. He's lucky to be walking around right now."

Tears burned in her eyes as she looked down at the fallen creature. "But what about the poor horse? Doesn't anybody care about him?"

Derrick shrugged. "Sure, it's a shame to lose a good animal, but you're going to have to toughen up, Jayne. This is cowboy country. Life is tough in the West. Animals come and go—"

"Speaking of going…" Jayne stood up. "I think I've had enough rodeo for today."

"Well, I haven't."

Jayne remained standing. Derrick's parents were sitting right behind them. They were probably staring at Jayne right now, wondering what was the matter with her. She decided to give Derrick ten seconds to change his mind. She waited, fixing her eyes on the brightly colored flags that flew over the arena. She knew that in another minute there would be tears running down her cheeks, and the last thing she needed was an audience this size. Not that many would notice. Most of the spectators were getting rowdy again, shouting and stomping their feet, anxious for the next contestant to ride.

She looked back down at Derrick. It was plain to see that he had no intention of leaving. "I'll see you later," she said, then turned and began to squeeze past many sets of denim-covered knees and cowboy boots, hoping that perhaps Derrick was following her. But when she turned her head, she could see from the corner of her eye that he hadn't budged. Finally, she reached the stairs, and there she paused for a moment to look back down at the arena. Maybe she was overreacting.

The horse was still lying there, motionless. She couldn't see if he was breathing or not, but she hoped he wasn't in pain. She swallowed hard and turned away again. As she entered the shadowy walkway, she noticed a tractor coming in with a flat trailer behind it. Her stomach twisted, thinking of the poor animal being carted away, and she hurried away from the arena and out to the parking lots. The announcer was already introducing the next saddle-bronc rider, and the crowd began to cheer wildly. How quickly they had forgotten the fallen horse.

Jayne felt hot tears run down her cheeks as she walked toward town. She felt foolish and childish. Maybe she just wasn't cut out for cowboy country, as Derrick had said. Maybe she just needed to "cowboy up" and go back and watch the rest of the rodeo. But with each step she took away from the rodeo grounds, she knew that she could not. She would not. She loved horses too much to be able to stand watching them like this.

Her obsession with horses had begun long ago. It had started innocently, with a gift from her Aunt May for her fifth birthday.

The sleek glass animal was a golden palomino with a long, flowing mane and its front hoof lifted proudly in the air. Soon after that, Jayne began collecting model horses, and then she began to draw pictures of horses, and it wasn't long until she was dreaming of horses. Every night for the next ten years she had prayed for a horse of her very own.

When she was fifteen, she got a job mucking out stalls for an equestrian center just outside of town—horse heaven. It was only a matter of days until she worked out a deal with the manager to trade work for the use of a horse and riding lessons. While she was earning her teaching degree, she promised herself that once she got a good job, she would buy a horse of her own.

Jayne walked across Main Street and sat down on a bench in front of the drugstore. Town was nearly deserted now with everyone over at the rodeo grounds. She took off her cowboy hat and wiped a wisp of dark hair off her brow. She leaned her head back and allowed the afternoon sun to pour down upon her face. Derrick's mother was always warning about skin cancer and telling her she should use sunscreen. Although she knew Mrs. Long was probably right, Jayne had the kind of skin that rarely burned so she didn't bother.

She readjusted the silver barrette that held her hair away from her face. The long, heavy ponytail was making her back too warm. Mrs. Long had suggested that she cut it, even offering to take Jayne to her own hairdresser. She said that Jayne's hair made her look too much like an Indian, but Jayne couldn't see what was wrong with that. Besides, Derrick seemed to like it. She closed her eyes and imagined that she was swimming in a shaded pool of water, with lush green things growing all around. The image was lovely, but it didn't cool her off.

The sun was starting to sink, but it was still hot out. Derrick had told her that Indian summers were common in this area, and even though it was September, she should count on a few more weeks of hot weather. She leaned forward, resting her elbows on her knees, and wondered what she should do now. She twirled the white straw cowboy hat around on her finger. It was a Stetson, a gift from Derrick's mother.

Jayne had only been in town for a couple of weeks, but already she was starting to feel at home. Until today, anyway. She wondered what Derrick's parents would say about her hasty exit. They were wheat ranchers and well known in the community. She had already met a number of their friends by attending barbecues, two parties, and now the town's biggest yearly event—the Paradise Roundup. Until today, she had been having a lot of fun here.

Maybe the horse lover in her was overly sensitive, but she was dusty and hot and tired, and she didn't want to go back to the rodeo. Besides, it bothered her that Derrick had shown so little concern; not just for the horse, but for her feelings. In less than three months they would be getting married, and she was beginning to wonder if they needed more time. Things between them hadn't felt quite right in the last few days. Derrick had been acting differently since returning to his hometown, but even more so recently. She couldn't put her finger on it, but something had changed. He seemed distant, almost cool. Perhaps it was just because he was back in his own stomping ground.

They really hadn't known each other very long. They had met less than a year ago, soon after she'd started her final year of college. Derrick had just graduated and was working in public relations, as well as helping out with the college group at her church. She had liked his outgoing and confident personality, and when she found out that his family had horses—lots of horses—she was more than a little interested. It wasn't long before they were dating, and then steadily. Even her conservative parents had liked him. Derrick had taken her to meet his parents during spring break, and on a trail ride, while she was actually in the saddle, he popped the question. Of course, she said yes.

In that moment, life had seemed just about perfect. She was not only marrying a great guy, but God had finally answered her prayer. She would have a horse. A lot of horses! On top of that, Derrick's dad was a golf buddy of the school superintendent, so landing a kindergarten teaching position had been a cinch. School would start in a few days, and Jayne had been spending several hours here and there over the past week setting up her classroom. Right now, life was just about perfect.

So why did she feel so perfectly lousy?

Two

———————◆———————

Derrick never mentioned the incident at the rodeo. She met him at his shiny new pickup, which had been a welcome-home present from his father, and they drove home in silence. It wasn't exactly a hostile silence, for Derrick had popped in a country music CD and hummed along. But just the same, it had been uncomfortable. She almost apologized for her emotional reaction, but she wanted him to apologize first. And it just didn't happen.

He parked the truck under the shade of an old locust tree. When Jayne climbed out, the ranch dogs ran up, barking out their friendly greetings. She reached down and scratched the golden Lab behind his ear for a moment, and when she straightened, Derrick was out of sight. He hadn't said a word.

Irritated, she turned and went to her room. At times like this, it was awkward being a guest in Derrick's parents' home, but she told herself this was only a lovers' quarrel. Fortunately, the house was huge and sprawling, making it easy to slip around without being noticed.

She flopped down on the neatly made bed. The blue-and-white bedspread felt cool against her bare arms. When she first came to stay with the Longs, she made the bed herself each morning. Then she realized that the maid was just remaking it anyway, so she decided to enjoy the unexpected luxury. The room and connecting bath were certainly nice enough, but everything, from the carpet to drapes to towels, was painfully matched in either royal blue or white, with no personal touches whatsoever. It reminded her of a hotel room. She had suggested to Derrick that perhaps she should find a place of her own before the wedding, but her finances were tight, so when Derrick insisted she stay here, she didn't protest too much. Soon they would have their own place, and she could insert as much personality as she liked.

Fortunately, on her first day here, Jayne had discovered a great hideout, and surprisingly, it was a place that Derrick seldom frequented. The horse barn provided a perfect haven, complete with all the wonderful smells of carefully maintained leather tack and fresh hay and grain.

Most important, there were horses there. It didn't even matter that quarter horses were not her favorites. She knew that quarter horses were considered the rancher's horse of choice, the cowboy's best friend, the working man's horse. And she respected that. Besides, these weren't average quarter horses; these were the best quarter horses that the Long money could buy. Their everyday horses were kept out in the pasture, but the ones in this barn got special treatment. Tommy Sanders took care of them. He was a weathered-looking old cowpoke, and he'd been at the Long ranch since the early sixties. He grumbled and complained about "them fancy, good-for-nothing" horses, but he was a meticulous caretaker, and Jayne suspected he loved horses just as much as she did. He was always willing to recite their pedigrees and point out the unique characteristics of each individual horse. And he called them all by name.

One day, Jayne had asked Tommy about trying out her English riding gear on one of the quarter horses. Tommy had a fit, launching into a long lecture adorned with colorful cowboy expletives about the foolishness and uselessness of English riding and that it was for sissified, citified blue-noses who didn't belong in this kind of country. She had pretended to take the ribbing in good humor, not wanting him to know that he had hurt her feelings. She didn't think he had meant to hurt her, but it was the last time she brought up the subject of riding English when Tommy Sanders was around.

The last few days of the Paradise Roundup passed uneventfully. On Sunday morning, Jayne went with Derrick and his parents to Cowboy Church. It was a Roundup tradition, and she had never been to anything quite like it. Local Christian cowboys led the service with a western-style worship, and then a couple of well-known cowboys shared their testimonies. The service was quite moving. Jayne wished they had it every Sunday, because it seemed more real than the stuffy church that Derrick's family usually attended.

After church, they went to a luncheon at the home of another wealthy cattle-owner friend of the Longs. There must have been over a hundred people there, but hardly anyone that Jayne knew, and no one seemed interested in knowing her. By the time they headed to the final rodeo performance that afternoon, her face felt tired from smiling, but she was determined to be a good sport today. Thankfully, no more serious accidents occurred. Derrick had become his easygoing self again, though perhaps a bit on the quiet side. With school starting the next day, Jayne had plenty to occupy her thoughts, so she didn't press him. That evening, as they were leaving the rodeo grounds, Derrick asked Jayne if she wanted to ride home with his folks while he met up with some old school buddies. Jayne willingly agreed. She had no desire to stay out late the night before her first day in the classroom, and she wanted to go over her lesson plans one more time.

The first day of school went surprisingly well. Her class of eighteen five-year-olds seemed to like her. Only Dylan Zimmer cried when his mother left him, but he seemed to be okay by snack time. Jayne took out her guitar and let the children take turns touching it and plucking the strings; and then she taught them a couple of songs. A number of the children were from the nearby reservation. Jayne had little experience with Native Americans, but she was drawn to their large, dark eyes and serious faces. As the week progressed, Jayne realized that it would take a little more work on her part to draw some of them out. They seemed a little more withdrawn and shy than the other children, but before long they started warming up to her. The only exception was Leah Bluefish, who was painfully shy. Jayne wasn't sure what it would take to win her over. She hoped that as Leah saw the rest of her playmates joining in and chattering away that she would follow along. By the end of the week, Jayne felt certain that she had been blessed with a wonderful group of children and that this would be a very good year.

Jayne had been so caught up with teaching and having everything set up just perfect in her classroom that she hardly noticed how little she had seen of Derrick this week. He had been absent at dinner for the past few days, but his mother always had a ready excuse, and Jayne had not questioned it. In fact, it had been something of a relief because it had allowed her to focus on her new job. She knew, too, that Derrick was still getting used to the routine of ranching. He hadn't decided yet whether to pursue another line of work or to devote himself full-time to helping his father run the ranch. His dad was pressuring him, and she didn't want to interfere.

But by Friday, Jayne was eager to spend some time with her

fiancé. She wanted to go out for dinner and to tell him about her week. She wanted to find out how his week had gone and how he was feeling about the ranch business. It was time for a good heart-to-heart.

She pulled into the driveway late Friday afternoon and looked around for his red pickup. When she didn't see it, she continued back to where the shops were located. She parked in front of the gas pump and looked around. There were all different kinds of farm machines and equipment, much of which still made no sense to her city-girl's eyes, but no Derrick. She looked to where a row of shiny silver combines stood at attention, like an army of robots ready to eat the wheat. Still no Derrick. She turned her car around and headed back to the house.

"Where's Derrick?" Jayne asked his mother, who was lounging on the back deck with a tall glass of iced tea.

Marge Long looked up with a troubled expression. "Sit down, dear," she said, in a voice that made Jayne feel uneasy. "Would you like some iced tea?"

"Sure, that sounds good." Jayne watched Marge's manicured hands as she gracefully poured amber-colored tea into a glass that had already been filled with ice and a wedge of lemon. It was almost as if she had been expecting Jayne to show up just now. Jayne sat down and took the glass, studying Marge for some sort of clue. But her expression was obscured by dark glasses and the shadow of an oversized sun hat.

"Jayne, there's something I need to tell you, and it's not going to be easy." Marge removed her glasses for a moment to peer at Jayne, then quickly replaced them. She directed her gaze to the field that stretched out before them like a calm sea of golden waves, rippling slightly in the afternoon breeze.

The Longs had one of the biggest spreads in the county.

Jayne had never heard the actual acreage count, but she knew it was in the thousands. The land had been in the family for generations and would all belong to Derrick one day.

Marge Long cleared her throat and began. "It's about Derrick. I've begged him to tell you himself, but he's being very obstinate. You know how he can be sometimes. Well, let me cut to the chase. Has Derrick ever mentioned Corky Galloway to you?"

Jayne shook her head, then took a sip of tea and forced herself to swallow.

"Corky and Derrick have been friends for just ages—why, they've known each other since sandbox days. The Galloways own a ranch on the east side; they're good friends of ours. Corky was rodeo queen, homecoming queen, prom queen, and, well, you name it, and the girl usually had a tiara on her head. She and Derrick dated off and on during high school. But when Corky went to college, she broke it off with Derrick so she could be free to play the field, so to speak. Then about two years ago, Corky got engaged to an older fellow in medical school."

She turned and looked at Jayne, then quickly glanced away. "I just can't believe Derrick didn't tell you any of this. Anyway, Corky was supposed to get married this fall, right after harvest-time. The invitations had already been sent out. But now Corky is back in town, and it seems she's called the whole thing off. Of course, that means she's available again." Mrs. Long laughed nervously but avoided looking at Jayne.

Despite the heat, Jayne felt cold all over. Her heart was pounding against her chest. She knew that her whole world was about to come crashing in around her. She just knew it.

Marge removed her dark glasses and looked at Jayne, actually meeting her eyes this time. Jayne expected to see some trace of sadness, maybe even pity—not that she wanted it. But to her surprise, it seemed as if Marge were pleased, even a bit smug.

"I'm so sorry to be the one to tell you, dear. But Paradise is such a small town, I didn't want you to hear it from someone else. As you can probably guess, Derrick and Corky are getting back together. You see, Derrick has spent every spare moment with her. It's only a matter of time—"

"Why hasn't he told me this himself?" Jayne struggled to keep her voice level.

"Oh, dear, I know it must be horrible for you. But better for this to happen now, rather than after you were married."

"Where is Derrick?" Jayne felt the words explode from her in what she was sure sounded like a shrill scream.

"No need to go to pieces, Jayne. These things happen. It's all for the best. Now, as far as your teaching job, I'm sure we can get Ron Whitfield to release you from your two-year contract—"

"You have no right to take away my job!"

"Well, I would hardly think that you'd want to stay."

Jayne stood and held her head high. "It's my decision, not yours. I'll pack up my things and be out of your way as soon as I find a place to live."

"You may stay as long as you need, Jayne. We're certainly not throwing you out."

Jayne shook her head as if she could shake off this horrible news. How could something like this be happening to her? And where in the world was Derrick? Could this possibly be some sort of cruel hoax his mother was pulling to break them up? Even as the thought formed, Jayne knew that what Marge had said was true.

"Just when did Derrick plan to let me in on this?" asked Jayne in a tightly controlled voice.

Marge frowned. "I don't know. I told him he needed to tell you right away, and we had a disagreement about that. He's gone to Portland for the weekend. He did say something about writing you a letter."

"A letter? A 'dear Jayne' letter?"

Marge nodded. "This is such an unfortunate situation, Jayne. If there's anything I can do to help, please feel free to ask."

"I'll be out of here by morning," said Jayne flatly, then turned and walked away. But instead of going back into the house, she walked out into the fields. She walked down the fence line until the house and all the farm buildings were nearly out of sight. Finally, she stopped at a place where a patch of wild grass grew. It was considered a weed by farmers, but it looked cool and green to her. She lay down there, shielded by its height.

She looked blankly at the clear canopy of blue sky stretching above her as silent tears streamed down her cheeks. She cried for a long time. After the tears had dried, she began to batter herself with unanswerable questions. Why had Derrick betrayed her like this? Why hadn't she seen it coming? What would she do now? Here she was, living in his parents' home, while Derrick was out running around with his old girlfriend. Was everyone laughing at her? How would she hold her head up in this town again? She was Derrick Long's castoff. He had brought her to Paradise, and now he didn't want her. He didn't even care enough to tell her to her face.

When she could stand the pounding questions no longer, she cried out to God. "Please," she said in a husky voice, "I need you more than ever right now. Please help me. I don't know what to do. It hurts so much, and I feel so worthless. I know you can turn bad things into good, but right now this looks hopeless. Please help me, God. Please." She could think of nothing more to say. She had never been good at flowery prayers; when she prayed, it was straight from the heart.

She folded her arms behind her head and looked up. A couple of sparrows flew high above her in the clear blue sky. It was so serene, so peaceful. Had God really heard her cries? She thought he had. She sighed deeply, then closed her eyes. Like a bird that had flown through a hurricane and then found shelter, she decided to rest in this peace.

When she awoke it was dark, but that fragile peace remained. She stood up and stretched, then began to walk back toward the house and barns. She didn't really want to go back, but where else could she go? Although the evening air was fresh and pleasant, she wasn't prepared to sleep under the stars. Her earlier sense of despair had diminished considerably. Somewhere inside her, she sensed that this breakup was probably for the best, even if she felt as though she were being torn apart. God still had his hand on her life, and although it seemed like a shambles right now, she needed, more than ever, to believe that God was still in control.

When she finally reached the lighted barn, she went inside to say good-bye to the horses. She gently stroked the soft muzzle of Sally Rose, the beautiful sorrel mare she had ridden so often. Suddenly she began to cry again. To her surprise, these racking sobs seemed to come from deep inside her, even deeper than before. But this time, it was not about losing Derrick. This was about losing the horses. All these beautiful horses would never belong to her now. She knew it was silly and superficial. It was a painful moment of truth, and it shamed her to admit, even to herself, that she had loved the horses more than she had ever loved Derrick. But it was true.

Perhaps it was she who needed to write the letter of apology.

THREE

J ayne found an apartment the very next day. The apartment complex was a dreary gray building, wedged between a grocery store and the railroad tracks. Not the best location perhaps, but one couldn't be choosy on such short notice. She spent the better part of her weekend moving things out of storage from one of the Longs' barns and into her new place. She hadn't been too worried about running into Derrick because she was certain that he was still hiding from her.

By Sunday night, she still hadn't heard from Derrick, and she began to think that might be a blessing of sorts. She had reached the point where she thought she might actually prefer a letter instead of a face-to-face confrontation. But her emotions rose and fell like a storm-swept sea. One moment she felt guilty for having almost married a man she had never really loved simply because he owned horses. The next moment, she felt furious for the way that he had brought her to Paradise and then so casually dumped her for his high-school sweetheart. No, she was not ready to see him yet.

She also wondered why she hadn't allowed Marge to get her out of her teaching contract, but now she was too embarrassed, or just too proud, to go and ask for help. But perhaps that too was for the best. She liked her job, she liked the children, and right now it was the only thing she had to hang on to. She hadn't called her parents yet. What could she tell them, that she'd been dumped for the rodeo queen? And besides, what could they do? Even this dingy little apartment was preferable to going back to her tiny room in her parents' house. No, there was no running back home. She had a job to do. And she would do it, at least until the end of the year. After that, maybe she would reconsider her options.

She hoped that she could budget her meager half-time salary to cover her living expenses. There could be no more careless spending or depending on the wealthy in-laws-to-be. Covering just the first month's rent and deposit had nearly cleaned her out. She had no idea how she would make it to the end of the month. She sat down on a box and looked around her. Bleak and dismal. Tears began to run down her face as she considered the hopelessness of this situation. No friends, no family nearby, no money.

Her eyes came to rest on the English saddle that was sitting in the corner, and suddenly she began to laugh. To think that only a couple of days ago she had been crying over horses. Now she had a nearly empty checking account, no food in the cupboard, and a strange town to live in. She leaned back against a stack of boxes and, closing her eyes, asked God to help her get through the month, or at least through these next few days. She felt as if she had prayed more in the past few days than she had all year long. But it was her lifeline and her only comfort right now.

The next day, it was a relief to go to work. The colorfully decorated walls of the classroom were much friendlier than her stark, box-filled apartment. The children were glad to see her, and the day went well. After her students went home at noon, she hung some leaf prints they had made that day on the windows. Then she puttered around, picking up books and toys and straightening things until the room looked almost perfect. Finally, she sat down in the low wooden rocker that she used for story time and sighed. How would she ever make it through a whole year? And what about the two-year contract?

"Hey, there," someone called from the hallway. Jayne looked up and saw Katherine Patawa, the other kindergarten teacher. They had first met at orientation, and later chatted briefly on the playground. Katherine seemed to be someone Jayne would like to know better. She had a soothing voice, and her dark eyes had a depth to them that suggested she was sincere and caring.

Katherine stepped into Jayne's classroom and looked around, nodding with approval. "Very nice, Jayne. For a first-year teacher, this room looks great."

"Thanks, Katherine. It's been fun doing it, and I have a feeling it's going to become my therapy." Jayne hadn't really meant to say that, but then she had never been a good one to guard her words.

Katherine frowned slightly. "Are you in need of therapy?"

Jayne forced a laugh. "Aren't we all from time to time?"

"I guess so. But you did look a little down today during recess. Everything going okay for you?" Katherine sat down on one of the small desks across from Jayne, her paisley skirt falling around her in long, graceful folds. She leaned forward slightly and looked intently into Jayne's eyes. Sympathy was one thing Jayne didn't need right now. Just a morsel of it would probably make her fall apart, and she wanted to appear strong and capable to this fellow teacher who seemed to have it all together.

"Well, I don't want to burden you with my personal life. But yes, I've had a pretty tough weekend."

"Trouble in Paradise?" Katherine's dark eyes flashed as if she knew something.

"Don't tell me—have you already heard?"

"Paradise is a small place."

Jayne leaned her head back. It figured. "Does everyone know?"

"That'd be my guess. Too many connections run through this town. And, if you haven't already figured it out, it's time that you learned that teachers talk."

Jayne sighed. "What exactly did you hear?"

"Oh, just the general stuff. Corky's back in town, minus one hunk of a diamond on a certain finger. She and Derrick have been seen together more than once."

Jayne groaned.

"I'm sorry, Jayne. I thought you knew all this." Katherine shook her head and looked at Jayne with concerned eyes. "I hope I haven't said too much. Frankly, I think you're too good for Derrick and his family."

Jayne forced another laugh. "Well, I think the Longs are glad to be rid of me. I wasn't in their class. Besides, it sounds as if Corky was meant to be Derrick's bride."

"You're lucky to have escaped them."

Jayne studied Katherine. She knew Katherine was Native American, but she really knew little else about her. She remembered that Derrick had treated Katherine coolly when they'd seen her at the Roundup parade. It had irked Jayne, but she had simply thought it was a guy thing. Katherine was quite a beauty, and Jayne supposed Derrick was just trying to appear as if he hadn't noticed.

"It sounds like you don't much care for the Long family, Katherine."

"As usual, I've probably said too much, Jayne. I'm sorry. I've been trying to be more forgiving and accepting. But some folks can be quite challenging. Before I say anything more, tell me, Jayne, is the engagement officially off?"

"It's as official as it can be for two people who haven't yet spoken of it. His mother told me the news, and I moved into my own apartment this weekend—" Suddenly, Jayne's voice began to break.

"I'm sorry, Jayne," said Katherine. She stepped closer and placed a hand on Jayne's shoulder. "Actually, I'm sorry that you've been hurt. But I'm not sorry that you and Derrick are not getting married. I probably shouldn't say that, but it's how I feel."

"It's okay. Actually, I think it's for the best. It's just hard knowing what to do next. I mean, here I am in a strange town with no one—"

"You're right about this being a strange town. But you're not alone. You've got someone, Jayne. You've got me." Katherine smiled.

"Thanks, Katherine. You have no idea how much that means to me."

"And can I give you a bit of advice—from someone who's been there?"

"Sure. I'll take any help I can get."

"Just take it one day at a time, Jayne. Like Jesus says, take care of today because tomorrow has enough trouble of its own."

"Are you a Christian, Katherine?"

Katherine nodded. "How about you?"

"Yes, but I think I have a lot of growing to do."

"Don't we all." Katherine looked at her watch. "Oops, I've got to get going. I need to pick up my daughter."

"You have a child? I didn't even know you were married."

Katherine smiled. "Well, you're old enough to know that people don't always have to be married to have kids. I had Autumn back in my old nonbelieving days, but I don't regret her one bit. Autumn has always been my little slice of sunshine."

"I'd love to meet her sometime."

"Don't worry, you will. How about if Autumn and I have you over for dinner?"

"That would be great."

"Is Thursday okay?"

"I'll put it in my date book," said Jayne with a grin. "Thanks, Katherine, for everything."

Katherine stood and tossed her thick black hair over her shoulder. "Hey, that's what friends are for."

Jayne had no desire to leave her classroom and return to her apartment. For some reason, the apartment had become like a dreary jail cell in her imagination. Having to spend each night there felt almost like a short prison sentence. The previous tenants had been smokers, and no matter how long she kept the windows open, it still reeked of stale smoke. But she could think of no more reasons to stay at school, so finally, she turned off the fluorescent lights and left.

On her way home from work, she stopped at the grocery store and bought ten packets of Ramen noodles for a dollar. These, along with a box of cornflakes, a couple of bananas, and some canned green beans, were going to have to get her through the week. In the apartment, she took a cool shower and slipped into a lightweight sundress. It was still like summer outside, and her place had no air-conditioning. She dug through one of her boxes until she located a saucepan, and began to prepare the Ramen noodles. Too bad she didn't need to lose weight; poverty might be a great way to force a diet. But she knew that she was thin enough. She remembered Katherine's advice—take it one day at a time. She gave thanks for her dinner of noodles, green beans, and an overripe banana; and after dinner she took a walk.

Somehow, she made it through the next two days—one day at a time. On Wednesday she offered to help the fifth-grade teacher, Audrey Richey, with some P. E. testing. Jayne was always looking for an excuse to linger after her students went home, and Audrey was pleased to have extra help with her oversized class. After the testing was done, Audrey invited Jayne to stop by her garden and help herself to an overabundance of produce. Jayne followed her home and was delighted to help pick two full grocery bags of fresh, sun-ripened vegetables. Some she would eat right away, but there would be plenty left to put up in her tiny freezer.

When she entered her apartment, she noticed a slim white envelope on the matted carpet just inside the door. She instantly recognized the neat handwriting, and her heart began to race with apprehension. It was from Derrick. After depositing the bags on the counter, she tore open the envelope. Several crisp green bills fell out. She picked them up in amazement. Each one was a hundred dollar bill—and there were six of them! Her first reaction was to thank God, but then her pride stepped in and she began to resent what seemed like payoff money. She opened the letter and read.

Dear Jayne,
You have no idea how difficult it is for me to write this letter to you. Let me start out by saying how sorry I am. I never planned for this to happen. Mother told me that she informed you about everything. You probably think I'm a coward, but I just didn't want to hurt you. When I saw Corky, I knew that what she and I used to have wasn't over. And when she told me she was no longer engaged, I knew that she and I were meant to be together.

But I am so sorry to do this to you, Jayne.

Mother said that you refused to give up your teaching position. I don't understand that, and I can't imagine why you would want to stay in Paradise after all this. But that's your choice. I know you must be in need of money, and I hope you will accept this as a small token of how sorry I am about everything. I know that God will help you to forgive me, Jayne. In time, I hope that you come to understand that this is for the best for both of us.

Sincerely,

Derrick

She folded the letter and returned it to the envelope. Looking around the dingy little apartment with too many boxes, she laughed. "For the best for both of us," she said. "Certainly it is for your best, Derrick Long." She didn't understand why it still hurt so much. Was it just her wounded pride? And why did she suddenly feel so bitter toward him? "Help me to forgive him, God, because right now I'd really rather spit in his face."

She cried herself to sleep that night. But when morning came, she felt surprisingly better. One day at a time.

Katherine met her in the hallway at school after their students had all gone home. "Don't forget about dinner tonight, Jayne. Did you find the directions I put on your desk?"

"They're in my purse. Don't worry, I'll be there at six o' clock sharp. It's not every night that I get a real meal."

Jayne quickly finished cleaning up. After much thought and prayer, she had decided to accept the money from Derrick as if God had given it to her, but she wanted to deposit it at the bank and then to budget it carefully. There was no telling how badly she'd need it before this year was over. Already she was toying with the idea of getting another part-time job to help her finances. Maybe Katherine would have some suggestions.

Just as Jayne was about to pull into the bank, she saw Derrick's pickup in the parking lot. She felt as though her heart had stopped, and instead of pulling into the drive-in lane, she kept going down the street, looking straight ahead. This was ridiculous. How would she ever get along in this small town if she was always watching for him, looking around every corner?

Suddenly she grew curious about this Corky who had captured Derrick's affections. She wondered what Corky was like. What did she look like? Probably curvy and gorgeous, with a wild mane of blond hair. Maybe a model type. Jayne imagined something akin to a Barbie doll with long legs and big blue eyes, and probably wearing a diamond studded crown. All at once Jayne felt dowdy and frumpy and plain. *Plain Jayne.* Not that anyone had ever called her "plain Jayne" before. In fact, people often told her she was attractive; commenting on her fine, smooth skin that tanned so easily, or how her long, almost black hair was such an amazing contrast to her blue eyes. But none of that seemed to mean anything now. She felt like a castoff, like a stray that no one wanted.

Feeling like a kicked dog, she drove back to her little apartment, slipped up the stairs, and hid away until it was time to get ready to go to Katherine's. She stood for a long time studying her reflection in the foggy bathroom mirror. There seemed to be nothing very interesting about her face. Normal eyes, nose, mouth. Even her hair was boring. She *was* a plain Jayne. She imagined the flamboyant Corky tossing her golden mane over her shoulder like a movie star. No wonder Derrick had picked Corky over her. Who wanted a plain Jayne?

FOUR

J ayne followed Katherine's directions and soon found herself driving through the reservation. It didn't look much
different from the surrounding area, but knowing that it
was the reservation gave her a strange feeling. Not bad, just different. In a way, she almost envied the Native Americans who
lived there. At least they had something solid they could call
their own—a place they could always return to, a home. She
didn't have anything like that. Not her parents' little tract
house, and definitely not her apartment.

She drove past numerous mobile homes, some later models
and many that looked like tin hot dogs. Some places looked
like dump sites, with old cars and broken-down machinery
strewn about unmowed yards. Then she came to a neatly kept
farm, or what Katherine had called a ranch. Katherine had told
her that her house was just beyond this spread. The ranch
property went on quite a ways, with pastures of horses and cattle
contentedly grazing alongside the road. Finally, Jayne saw a
driveway with Katherine's last name on the mailbox at the
end. She pulled in and parked in front of an old two-story
house. Unlike many of the homes she had just seen, this one
was in good repair, with fresh paint. The neatly landscaped
yard reminded Jayne of an old-English garden, with wisteria
climbing up the porch and flower beds overflowing with color.

Katherine waved from the front porch. "You found us!" A
smiling yellow Lab trotted out to meet Jayne, its tail wagging in
welcome.

"That's Shamee," said Katherine. "She's a people lover."

Jayne reached down to scratch the dog behind the ear. "Nice to meet you, Shamee." In return she received a sloppy lick on the hand.

Katherine laughed. "Okay, Shamee, now you've baptized her. Come here, girl."

Jayne turned around and gazed at the yard. "Katherine, this is beautiful. I feel like I've come to an oasis. Your yard is absolutely wonderful."

"Thanks. We enjoy it. Jayne, this is my daughter, Autumn." Jayne looked up to the porch. Standing next to Katherine was a slim girl who looked to be about ten or eleven. Katherine wrapped her arm around the girl's shoulders and smiled proudly.

"It's a pleasure to meet you, Autumn," said Jayne as she stepped onto the porch.

"Hi, Jayne," said Autumn. She smiled shyly. Her teeth were very crooked, and Jayne wondered if that contributed to her shyness.

"What grade are you in?" asked Jayne.

"Fifth. I'm in Mr. Worth's class."

"He seems like a nice person. Do you like him?"

Autumn nodded hesitantly. "But it's the first time I've had a man for a teacher."

"I remember the first man I had for a teacher. I was in fifth grade, too. His name was Mr. Glenn, and he was short and bald, but after I got to know him, I really liked him. In fact, I think he was one of my favorite teachers."

Autumn smiled again, wider this time. Jayne remembered that Katherine had called Autumn her "sunshine." When she smiled like that, it was as if her whole face lit up.

"Can I help you in the kitchen, Katherine?"

"We've already decided to put you in charge of the salad," said Katherine with a sly wink. "Neither of us likes doing salads very much."

Jayne oohed and aahed over the interior of Katherine's house. It was very homey, with large, overstuffed furniture accented by a nice selection of antiques, handmade pottery, and colorful handwoven rugs. "Your place is perfect," said Jayne as they worked on dinner. "If you ever quit teaching, maybe you should go into interior design."

Katherine laughed. "The problem is, I could only do houses that look like this."

"Nothing wrong with that." Jayne tore pieces of dark green lettuce and dropped them into a big wooden bowl. She noticed that Shamee had joined them in the kitchen, her nails clicking on the tiled floor. The dog plopped down in a corner, but she watched them closely and almost seemed to listen to their conversation.

Dinner was a delight. Jayne concentrated on Katherine and Autumn, trying to push from her mind all the unhappy thoughts that had plagued her earlier in the afternoon. They played Scrabble after dinner, then Autumn went upstairs to do her homework.

"Katherine, I didn't think you were old enough to have a ten-year-old daughter," said Jayne as she helped clean up the dinner dishes. "I thought you were about the same age as me."

"Just how old do you think I am?"

"Well, I'm almost twenty-four. I would have guessed you might be a year or two older since you've been teaching a couple years already."

Katherine nodded. "I had Autumn when I was only sixteen.

My mother helped raise Autumn so that I could finish high school. Then I went to college and got my credential, and this is my third year of teaching."

"That's great that you didn't let having a child stop your education."

"Yes, I was determined to have a better life. In fact, back then I thought an education would be my ticket away from here. Actually, it was."

"Then what happened?"

"God told me to come back."

Jayne nodded, not knowing quite how to respond to that. She assumed that coming back was a good thing, but she wasn't sure. "So if you grew up around here, you must have known Derrick in school." Jayne instantly wished she hadn't brought him up. Why ruin such a nice evening?

"We weren't friends, but we were in the same class. Do you want to see my yearbook?"

"Sure." Jayne wasn't really sure that she did, but what could it hurt?

Katherine pulled out a dark red book. "This was from our senior year." She flipped through some pages and then pointed to a photograph. "There he is. Doesn't really look all that different, does he?"

Jayne studied the picture. Derrick's hair and features did look very much the same as they did now, but she noticed he was wearing a self-satisfied, almost smug expression. One she had seen before. Why hadn't she realized it for what it was? "You know, I haven't actually seen or talked to him since I moved out of his parents' house."

"You're kidding!"

"Weird, huh?"

"I'd say so. But I'm not surprised. Jayne, I don't mean to sound insensitive, but you should be relieved to be out of there. Do you mind me saying that?"

"No, not really. I guess I am relieved, but I'm still sort of in shock. And I'm still feeling hurt. Today I was imagining how gorgeous Corky must be—since she was queen of everything and all. I was feeling like a real dog this afternoon." Jayne tried to laugh. "A real plain Jayne."

Katherine burst into laughter, throwing her head back. "You must be insane. First of all, you're beautiful—I thought that the minute I saw you. But more than just outward beauty, you have a warmth, a kindness, a heart—"

Jayne laughed. "Katherine, you don't have to flatter—"

"No, let me finish. I won't go on about your looks because when you're feeling better about all this, you'll see yourself for who you are; but do let me say this: I'm proud to be Native American. I think we're a beautiful people, and when I saw you with your straight, thick hair, I thought you were one of us. Not that it matters that you're not, but I mean that as a compliment."

"Thanks. I feel very flattered." Shamee came over and flopped her head onto Jayne's lap as if to confirm her owner's words. It seemed silly to care so much about her appearance, but suddenly she felt so much better.

"But that's not all." Katherine grinned. "Now I hate it when women sound catty, and I don't mean to, but have you ever actually *seen* Corky?"

Jayne shook her head, and Katherine began flipping through the annual again. She held up a picture of a group of cheerleaders, all dressed alike in red-and-white uniforms. "Okay, which one do you think is her?"

Jayne studied the smiling faces of the group of girls, then

finally pointed to the tall one on the end. She had a mane of beautiful blond hair and big blue eyes, very close to the way Jayne had pictured Corky.

Katherine laughed. "That's Jenny Jacobs—she's a good friend of mine." She pointed to a stocky redheaded girl in the center. "That's Corky Galloway."

Jayne stared at the strange girl with a slightly turned-up nose, smattering of freckles, and bushy red hair. "You're kidding! I mean, she's cute, but I can't believe that's Corky Galloway."

"Like I said, I don't want to be catty." Katherine closed the book. "But Derrick isn't going after her for her looks."

"What is it then?"

"I don't know. I think they really did like each other in high school. Her parents are good friends with the Longs. They have a social position in the town. Who knows. Just be thankful you got out when you did."

Jayne nodded. "Thanks, Katherine."

"For what?" Katherine's brows lifted slightly over her dark brown eyes.

"For being a friend. And boy, do I need a friend."

Katherine smiled. "So, do you like horse shows?"

"Well, yes, as a matter of fact, I'm quite fond of horses. Why?"

"Because Autumn is showing her gelding in a show on Saturday. Want to come? It's about an hour away, in a little town called Henley."

"I'd love to."

"Great, and if you want to dress western, feel free—everyone does."

"Sounds like fun."

After chatting for a while longer, Jayne finally thanked

Katherine for dinner and then headed for home. On the way back to her apartment, she thanked God for Katherine's friendship. She was like a ray of hope in what seemed like a depressing world right now.

On Saturday morning, Jayne got up early to go to the horse show. She was thankful to have something to keep her busy. She donned a red gingham shirt with pearl snaps and Wrangler jeans along with her Roper boots, the ones that Derrick had said didn't look as western as regular cowboy boots. At first she didn't want to wear the trophy belt that Derrick had given to her, but then decided she didn't care—it was just a thing. Not like the diamond engagement ring that she had returned to its box and mailed back to Derrick only a few days ago. She pulled her hair into a long ponytail and put on her white straw hat, then glanced at the long, lean cowgirl she saw in the mirror and smiled. Not bad. She remembered how even Derrick used to comment on how she made "one good-looking cowgirl."

When she realized she still had some time before she had to leave for the show, Jayne looked around at the still unpacked boxes in her apartment and wondered which one contained her quilting things. Ever since the dinner at Katherine's, she had wanted to find a small lap quilt she had put together last year. She knew the color and design would look perfect with Katherine's decor, and she wanted to give it to her as a token of friendship and gratitude.

After digging through several boxes, she finally found the right one. She pulled out many of the quilted items she had made, fingering the textures and admiring the colors and designs. Her Aunt May had taught her to quilt as a teen. In the past year, Jayne had designed some new patterns using colors and fabrics that Derrick had helped her pick out. They were supposed to have been for their newlywed home. Now she looked at the items and wondered if she should give them all away. They weren't painful reminders, but they were certainly not pleasant, either. She located the lap quilt on the bottom of the box. She had made the piece before meeting Derrick, and she was quite fond of it. But that made it even more special as a gift, and she felt certain that Katherine would appreciate it.

Katherine and Autumn were all ready to go when Jayne arrived, so she decided to give Katherine the quilt later. She rode with them in their old pickup truck, which was hitched to a rickety single-horse trailer. Jayne tried not to compare Katherine's rig to the state-of-the-art trucks and trailers sitting around at the Long Ranch. She would much rather ride in a clunker with Katherine than be with Derrick in his loaded power-stroke diesel extended cab any day.

"Autumn, you look so nice in your vest and tie," said Jayne as Katherine opened up the back of the trailer. "Tell me all about your horse. What's his name?"

"Well, his name is Red Pepper, but I call him Red."

Jayne stroked the neck of the sorrel. "Red's a perfect name. He's a beautiful horse, Autumn."

"He's a great-grandson of Little Peppy," said Autumn proudly. "Red just turned six last spring. I've had him since I was seven. We get along pretty good." Like a mother getting her child ready for a party, Autumn smoothed and straightened his mane.

"What exactly will you be doing to show your horse?" asked Jayne.

"I'm in three classes. Western pleasure, showmanship halter, and trail. I like trail the best."

"That sounds like fun. I don't know much about western horse shows, but I used to participate in some small equestrian shows that the people I worked for held. I liked to do dressage, but I never considered myself an expert."

"I'd like to learn to ride English," said Katherine.

"Really, even around here in cowboy country?" Jayne looked over at her friend curiously, remembering what Tommy Sanders had said about English.

Katherine laughed. "Maybe I'd like a different way to ride since they all treat me differently anyway."

"You'd probably like riding English. The saddles are much lighter and you can feel the horse better. It can be a challenge if you've only ridden western, but if you like riding bareback, you'd probably be a natural."

After several attempts, they got Red loaded into the trailer.

"He can be sort of fussy about loading," explained Autumn as they headed down the driveway.

"I knew a horse that had to be drugged in order to travel," said Jayne. "His name was Obsidian, but we all called him Obstinate."

After an hour's drive, they arrived at the Henley arena. "You can go look around if you want to, Jayne," said Katherine. "I'll help Autumn unload Red and get them settled. Then I'll meet you in the stands."

Jayne wandered off, watching as people unloaded horses. Suddenly she wondered if any Long quarter horses might be here. She hoped not. This seemed like a pretty small-scale horse show; it was probably beneath the Longs to show in a little town like this. As she was waiting in line for coffee, she saw a sign for raffle tickets. Apparently they were giving away a horse. *Giving away a horse!* She quickly abandoned the coffee line to find out where she could buy a raffle ticket.

"Over at the west gate," said a portly woman in full western attire. "It's ten bucks a ticket." Jayne hurried over to the gate. Perhaps she was being silly; right now even ten dollars was a lot. She had been trying to be very frugal. But to pass up a chance to win a horse—unthinkable. She purchased her ticket and slipped it into her pocket.

"Is the horse somewhere around here?" she asked.

"You betcha," said the man as he dropped the other half of her ticket into the bucket. "His name is Bailey, and he's out on the east end, behind the arena." The man pointed to the opposite side of the arena.

Jayne thanked him and began heading that direction. She glanced around to see if Katherine had found a seat yet, but didn't see her. When Jayne reached the east end, she went outside to see a temporary corral set up. The only horse inside was a bay gelding. A couple of men were standing around, scuffing their toes in the dirt and chuckling about the freebie horse. She glanced at the horse; his head was down, almost as if he could hear their comments and was ashamed. She walked around to where she could see his face. She clicked her tongue softly and reached out her hand. He slowly walked over and nudged her hand, looking up at her with dark, soulful eyes filled with intelligence. Her heart melted.

"I can't believe ol' Bender would allow one of his prize mares to be bred by an A-rab," snickered a potbellied cowboy.

"Yeah, those A-rabs are a useless bunch," chuckled the other cowboy. "I hear they're hotheaded, flighty things."

"A couple years back, Bender was boarding an A-rab stallion," said the potbellied cowboy. "He sure didn't keep him around for long—guess this is why."

The other cowboy burst into laughter. "Yeah, I betcha that A-rab got hold of one of Bender's mares. No wonder this give-away horse is a gelding!"

Jayne stared at the two men. She wanted to say something, anything. But men like that didn't deserve to be reasoned with.

She turned her focus back to Bailey. He nuzzled her again, looking into her eyes as if asking her to rescue him from his horrible life and people who couldn't appreciate him for who he was. Jayne pulled out her billfold and checked to see how many raffle tickets she could possibly afford. She only had enough cash for three more. She stroked his nose. "I'll do what I can, Bailey."

The men stopped their talk and stared at her. "You ain't gonna try and win that half-breed, are ya?" said Potbelly.

She looked him squarely in the eye and said, "All creatures are precious in God's eyes, and I would be proud to own this horse." Then she turned on the heel of her boot and began to march back to the raffle table. As she walked to the other side of the arena, she heard the announcer introducing the first event. She hoped it wasn't Autumn's. She glanced up to the stands and saw Katherine waving frantically. Jayne decided she should go tell Katherine what she was up to and find out when Autumn's event would start.

"I've been looking all over for you," said Katherine as she scooted over to make room. "Autumn is in the next class."

Jayne sat down, deciding to wait until Autumn's class was over before she went back down to buy her other raffle tickets. She listened impatiently as Katherine described what an ordeal they had experienced when they tried to get Red out of the trailer. He was still not used to backing out and had nearly kicked Autumn in the leg. "Thank goodness she jumped in time. It's not really his fault. We probably just need to practice going in and out with him more."

"I bought a raffle ticket for the horse," said Jayne. She wondered what Katherine would think.

Katherine laughed. "Just what you need."

Jayne didn't respond. She knew that Katherine didn't mean

it in a bad way. And she was right, Jayne's life was a mess right now. How could getting a horse help? It was probably a crazy thought to buy four raffle tickets for a chance to win a horse she had no way of caring for. But still—

"Okay, before we move on to the next event, we are going to raffle off the Bender gelding. This isn't something we normally do, and we want you folks to know that the raffle-ticket money will be donated to the Ronald McDonald house in Paradise. Of course, Greg Bender will probably take a little tax write-off." The crowd chuckled. "And let's not forget to acknowledge the Riverview Veterinary Clinic for their generous donation. Thanks, Dr. Jim…"

Katherine leaned over and whispered to Jayne. "I heard part of the deal was that Bender would only donate the horse if they would cover the gelding fee. He didn't want the horse to sire any foals."

Jayne could hardly listen. She felt sick at the way Bailey had been treated, and she wanted him now more than ever. But it was too late to get those extra tickets.

"So get out your ticket stubs, and let's give away a horse," the announcer finished. He started to read the number.

"Where's your ticket?" asked Katherine.

With a blank stare, Jayne pulled her ticket out of her pocket. Then instead of looking at the ticket's number, she closed her eyes and prayed for a horse—just as she had as a child. But not just any horse. She wanted Bailey.

"Jayne!" Katherine screamed as she pulled the ticket from her hand. "You won! Jayne, you won a horse!"

Jayne opened her eyes and looked at Katherine in amazement. "What?"

"I said you won!"

People all around her were watching now, smiling and congratulating her.

"Go get your horse, cowgirl," said an older man in a ten-gallon hat.

"Go on, Jayne," said Katherine. "You've got yourself a horse."

Somehow Jayne made it down the steps and to the place where the man selling the raffle tickets was standing. He shook her hand and handed her an envelope full of papers. Then he had her sign some forms. She just blindly scrawled her name, too excited to read them, but he assured her they were just ordinary ownership forms. She realized she probably would have signed anything to get her horse.

"He's all yours, little lady," said the man with a wide smile. Then in a quieter voice he added, "And no matter what some folks think, that there is one heck of a good horse. He's well bred and good natured. What more can you ask for? Take care now."

She smiled at him. "Thank you so much. I think he's an absolutely wonderful horse. Thank you. Thank you!"

She began to walk back to her seat. "I can't believe it," she said. "Thank you, Lord. Thank you!"

"Say, miss," said a portly woman. "Do you mind me asking how many raffle tickets you bought to win that horse?"

Jayne smiled. "Only one."

The woman punched the man next to her. "And you bought ten!"

"And now for our western pleasure novice class," said the announcer. "Will the participants please enter the ring." He continued to talk, but Jayne could hardly listen as she forced herself back up the steps to join Katherine. She wanted to go outside and hug Bailey, but after all, she had come to see Autumn compete.

"That's so incredible, Jayne!" said Katherine, patting her on the back. "I can't believe it. Congratulations." She turned back to the stadium. "Watch, here comes Autumn."

Jayne's eyes could barely focus on Autumn's event, but she noticed that Red was moving perfectly and Autumn was sitting correctly. Jayne felt certain that if Autumn had only smiled, she might have gotten the blue ribbon. But Jayne clapped loudly with Katherine when Autumn took second place in her class. She was presented with a big red ribbon and a silver buckle. Katherine and Jayne met her down at the stable, and Katherine pulled out a camera and took several shots. Jayne congratulated Autumn for her award, then excitedly told her about winning the raffle.

"Jayne, that's great!" squealed Autumn. "Now we can all go riding together! It'll be an hour before my next class. Can I see him?" They quickly got Red settled in an empty stall, and the three of them went to pay their regards to Jayne's new horse.

"I think he's a lovely horse," said Autumn as she stroked Bailey's sleek flank.

"Some of the men were saying that being half-Arabian is a horrible thing, but I could care less. In fact, I've always admired Arabians. I happen to think Bailey's the handsomest, sweetest, most wonderful horse in the world."

Katherine laughed. "Sounds like love at first sight."

Jayne sighed as she stroked his dark mane. "It was."

"Do you want to come back and watch the rest of the show with us, or would you rather stay out here and swoon?" asked Katherine.

Jayne felt silly admitting it, but she wanted to stay with her horse. "Swooning sounds good to me," she said. "If you don't mind, I'll catch up with you later."

Katherine just chuckled. "I don't blame you a bit. This is so amazing!"

Jayne stayed with Bailey for quite a while, and then went back to check on the show, hoping that maybe she'd catch a glimpse of Autumn on Red. But after only a few minutes, she wanted to return to Bailey. After repeating this cycle several times, she began to wonder if this was how it felt to have a newborn baby. She couldn't stand to have Bailey out of her sight for even a few minutes. And she couldn't wipe the silly grin off her face. Strangers came up and congratulated her.

A teenaged girl walked up and looked longingly at Bailey. "Did you have to buy a lot of tickets to get him?" asked the girl.

"No, I only bought one."

"No kidding?"

"I wanted to buy more, but I didn't get there in time."

"Wow, you must be lucky."

"Actually, I have to give God the credit. I was really praying to win."

The girl nodded. "I've been praying for a horse, too."

Jayne smiled and ran her hand down Bailey's neck. "Well, don't stop. I had to pray for a long time before I got this one. But he's worth the wait."

At last the show was over, and Katherine and Autumn came out to check on Jayne and Bailey. Autumn had gotten a blue ribbon for her trail class. She was beaming.

"Congratulations, Autumn. I guess this has been a great day for both of us," said Jayne. "I'm still floating on a cloud."

"Well," said Katherine with a creased brow, "it may be time to climb off your cloud and figure some things out. I was just wondering, Jayne, where exactly are you going to keep him? Your apartment is a little small."

Jayne frowned. She hadn't even thought about that yet. "Where does Autumn keep her horse?"

Now Katherine frowned. "Autumn and I both keep our horses with my uncle. I would offer to ask about yours, but—" Katherine paused. "Well, Black Hawk isn't very fond of—well, people who aren't Indian. He's a little prejudiced that way. I'm sorry."

Jayne nodded. "No, it's okay. This is my problem, not yours. I don't suppose you have enough land to keep horses?"

"Not really. And what little I have isn't even fenced."

"Hey, Mom, how about Harris?" said Autumn.

"Good idea, Autumn," said Katherine. "In fact, that's a great idea! Harris would be perfect."

"Who's Harris?" asked Jayne.

"My neighbor. He's a rancher, and he has a fair amount of pasture. Plus he grows his own hay so you could buy it from him and not have to get it delivered. Harris would be just perfect. I'll bet he'd even come over with his trailer and pick Bailey up. How about if I give you Harris's number; you could give him a call while we're loading Red. Just tell him that I told you about him."

"Thanks, Katherine. You are truly a godsend." After Katherine left, Jayne wondered how much it would cost to board and feed a horse. Perhaps she would need to get that part-time job now. But that was okay. She looked into Bailey's eyes.

"You and I are going to be best friends, Bailey. I don't care if I have to sling burgers or dig ditches to buy your oats and hay. Don't worry, I'll always take care of you."

Jayne found a pay phone and dialed the number, wondering what sort of person this Harris was. If Katherine thought he'd be willing to help her, he must be nice. The phone rang again and again, but Jayne wasn't willing to give up easily.

"Hello?" a gruff masculine voice said finally.

"Is this Harris?"

"Yeah."

"Hi. I'm sorry to disturb you, but my friend Katherine Patawa gave me your name. She said that I might be able to rent some pasture from you. You see, I just got a horse and—"

"Well, I'm picky about who I rent pasture to. Vaccinations need to be current. Pay on time or you're out. You'll have to sign a liability release. I expect the owners to take full responsibility for their animals, and I don't put up with neglect."

"You won't have to worry about neglect. This horse means a lot to me."

He chuckled. "Okay. If Katherine recommends you, you must be all right. When do you want to bring him by?"

Jayne pressed her lips together. "Uh, I don't exactly have a way to bring him to you."

"You don't have a trailer?"

"No. You see, this is the first time I've actually owned a horse.…"

"I see." His voice sounded suspicious. "So, do you know anything about horses?"

"Yes, I've worked with horses a lot. But this is the first time—"

"Right, I understand. Do you want me to come pick him up?"

"Would it be too much trouble? I hate to inconvenience you. And I'll certainly pay you for your gas and your time and whatever."

He made a sound that sounded like a cross between a grunt and a groan. "Yeah, I suppose I could come. Where are you, anyway?"

She quickly told him, making it clear how much she appreciated his help, how grateful she was, and how she would reimburse him, until he abruptly cut her off. She hung up the phone and sighed. Normally she would refuse to grovel and beg like that, but she would gladly sacrifice her pride for Bailey.

Katherine pulled up with the loaded trailer behind her. "Did you get hold of him?" she called from the open window.

"Yes, he's coming."

"Harris is a good ol' coot. Give me a call after you get Bailey unloaded and settled in, and I'll come by and pick you up."

FIVE

◆

J ayne didn't really mind that it took Harris a couple of
hours to arrive. It gave her time to walk Bailey around
and get better acquainted. He was very gentle and trusting, and it was almost as if they were old friends. She kept
thinking it was a dream, but then she would stroke his coat
and smell his wonderful, earthy horse smell, and she knew it
was for real. Again and again, she thanked God for this amazing and unexpected blessing. If God could give her a beautiful
gift like this, then God could surely help her to keep and care
for him.

After a while, the parking lot was nearly deserted. Jayne
found a shady area with a water trough and an old wooden
bench and sat down. The afternoon shadows were growing
longer, and although it had been a hot day, she could almost
smell autumn in the air. For the first time that day, she thought
of Derrick and almost laughed aloud. What would he think of
her having a horse? Not that she cared. But there was a sense of
satisfaction in knowing that she could own a horse without
being owned by Derrick. She had never thought of it in those
words before, but that was how she had felt—as if, when she
had married him, he and his family would slowly come to own
her. She sighed, thankful to be free.

She looked toward the parking lot but saw no sign of anyone bringing in a horse trailer. She wondered what this Harris
was like. She imagined a grizzled old farmer in his fifties,
chewing on a piece of hay. She'd liked what he had said about

wanting owners to take good care of their animals. She was glad to know Bailey would be staying with someone who obviously valued horses. Just then, a dark blue pickup pulling a shiny aluminum horse trailer pulled into the parking lot. She stood up. Bailey lifted his head and looked at her, as if he understood he was about to go home. She picked up the lead and walked hesitantly toward the rig. When a tall, lean cowboy climbed out, she stopped. This man was much too young to be Harris.

"Are you Katherine's friend?" he called out.

"Yes!" Surprised, she started walking toward him again. "You must be Harris."

"That's right. Sorry, I don't remember if you told me your name or not."

"I'm Jayne Morgan." She smiled brightly. "And you have no idea how thankful I am that you could come and help me like this."

He took off his hat and shook her hand, keeping his clear blue eyes steadily on hers the whole time. "Pleasure to meet you, Jayne." She felt her cheeks grow warm and hoped he didn't notice. "And any friend of Katherine's is a friend of mine. She's a first-rate neighbor." At last he took his eyes off her and looked over at Bailey. Suddenly his smile faded, and his forehead creased slightly. "This your horse?"

His tone put her on the defense. "Yes, this is Bailey."

Harris shook his head slowly like a doctor about to announce a very dismal prognosis. "This looks like an Arab to me."

Jayne paused, trying to compose herself. She didn't want to burn this bridge. Bailey needed a good place to stay, so she needed Harris right now. Perhaps she could make him appreciate Bailey. "Yes, he's registered as half-Arabian, but he's out of a

Bender quarter horse, and a direct descendant of Poco Bueno. I think he's beautiful. Look how fine his head is, and his eyes are so expressive. I think he's very intelligent."

"Is this that raffle pony that belonged to Bender?"

"Yes, he is." Jayne twisted a strand of Bailey's dark mane between her fingers. "I won him. Can you believe it?"

Harris shook his head again and made a noise that sounded like a grunt. "You sure you want to keep him?"

"Of course." She looked up at Harris with surprise. How could he even question that? "You see, Harris, since I was a little girl, I have prayed for a horse. It was all I ever dreamed of. And recently, well, my life has taken some hard turns. I really believe that God gave me this horse today. Can you understand that?"

"I suppose so." Harris's eyes twinkled ever so slightly, then he shrugged. "But I can't say I'm real excited about having an Arab on my property. A cowboy's got his pride. But I guess I'm big enough to take the abuse that this will get me."

"Really?" Jayne looked at him with wide eyes. "Do they take horses that seriously around here?"

"I can see you're new in town, Jayne. You've got a lot to learn. Well, let's get him loaded. Hopefully he's not a greenhorn when it comes to loading. I've never had anything to do with Arabs, but I've heard they can be temperamental beasts."

Jayne bit her tongue and waited as Harris took the lead and led Bailey into the sturdy trailer. Fortunately, Bailey loaded quickly and easily. Jayne was careful not to gloat and didn't mention how difficult Autumn's quarter horse had been earlier today. She was just thankful to be on their way.

Jayne looked over at Harris as they traveled down the highway. He wasn't anything like she had imagined. And despite his attitude toward her horse, or Arabians in general, she liked him. Sandy blond waves of hair showed beneath his dusty straw cowboy hat. His profile was strong and interesting. He had the kind of face that looked as if it had been chiseled: high cheekbones; strong jaw; straight, almost sharp, nose. He would make a good hero in a cowboy movie. She would guess by the weathered lines fanning out from his eyes that he was in his thirties, but he could just as easily be in his twenties. He had the kind of looks that concealed age. She stole a quick look at his left hand, there was no trace of a wedding band. But then working men often took off their rings for safety's sake. And why should she care anyway?

He turned and glanced at her. "So, how long have you been in town?"

"I moved out here just a few weeks ago."

"What brings you to this part of the country?"

She thought for a moment. She had no desire to disclose any personal issues. "I got a teaching job at Applegate Elementary."

"Really? That's where I went to school when I was a kid. That must be how you met Katherine."

"Yes. She's about the only friend I have right now."

"She's a good one to hang on to."

Jayne wondered if Harris and Katherine might be involved. If that were the case, Jayne would need to be careful and not intrude—no matter how attractive she thought Harris was. "I take it you grew up here?"

"Fifth generation."

"Wow, that's a long time."

"Uh-huh. Deep roots. Of course, the ranch I'm working only goes back to my dad. I've got a cousin on the north end of town who has the original family ranch. But I like where I'm at just fine."

"Is your ranch actually on the reservation?"

"Yes. My dad bought land from the tribe back in the late sixties. I was just a baby then, so all my childhood memories are on that farm."

"Do you run it by yourself?"

"No, it's sort of a family operation. But my dad is slowing down a lot these days...." His voice trailed off. "Where are you from? I mean, before you moved here."

"The Portland area. I sure don't miss the traffic."

He laughed. "Boy, I wouldn't last a week over there. Once in a blue moon I drive over to do errands, but I can't wait to get out of the city. It makes me feel so claustrophobic."

"I know what you mean. Even though I grew up there, I never realized how many things I disliked. When I first came to Eastern Oregon, all I could do was look at the skies and drink it in. I love stretching my eyes to see all the horizons. That's something you can't do on the other side of the mountains."

"Too many billboards and buildings. Even too many trees."

"Yes. And even though I like trees, I would happily trade them for these wide, clear blue skies."

"Looks like you have. At least for now, anyway."

She looked out the window at the rolling hills of golden grain. "I know this isn't the Midwest, but it sure feels like the heartland to me."

"Well, there's plenty of farming in this country. We grow a lot of wheat, but there are other crops as well. And there are a lot of cattle ranchers, too. I'm sure most Eastern Oregon farmers would think of this as the heartland."

They were on the reservation now. Once again, Jayne found herself studying her surroundings. She couldn't get over the feeling she had just entered into another culture, although she couldn't explain why. It didn't look that different. Sure, many of the yards were cluttered with old vehicles and broken-down machinery, but she knew they had a different set of values when it came to these things. She was interested in how they lived, what was important to them, and their history. Her interest had probably started with the reservation children in her class. Then, of course, there were Katherine and Autumn, although they seemed no different than anyone else. In fact, in many ways, she and Katherine were very much alike.

"What's it like living on the reservation?" she asked.

Harris looked as though he were thinking seriously about the question. "I don't know. I guess since I've lived here all my life I take a lot of things for granted."

"Do you have a lot of Native Americans for friends?"

He laughed. "Depends on what you mean by 'friends.'"

"You know, do you do things with them, go to their homes, have them come to yours...."

"No. Can't say as I do. Except Katherine, but she's not your typical Native American."

"What do you mean?"

"Well, Katherine has made something of her life. She's pulled herself up by her bootstraps, got educated, and now she supports herself and her daughter. She doesn't have to live on the reservation. She wants to. I respect that."

"Meaning you don't respect the others?"

"I wouldn't put it like that."

"How would you put it?"

He turned and looked at her. She couldn't tell if he was getting exasperated at her questions or just confused.

"I'm sorry, Harris. I must sound pretty nosy. I guess I'm just curious, trying to understand how life is around here. I know some people who live here...." She paused, not wanting to mention the Longs' name or her connection with them. "Anyway, they seemed to put down the Native Americans. Sort of like they were prejudiced. Their attitude seems so unfair, and it really caught me off guard."

Harris still didn't say anything, but she could tell by his face that he was thinking about her words, and he seemed a little perplexed. She wondered if she had stepped on his toes. Why hadn't she just kept quiet? After all, this man was helping her transport her horse and providing pasture space for him to stay; the very least she could do was to be congenial.

He pulled into the long driveway of the nice-looking ranch she had admired on her way to Katherine's. She wanted to ask him how many acres he had but had already been told that one should not ask a rancher how big his spread was. The fence line seemed to go back a long way, at least as far as her eye could see. Of course, by Long standards, it was probably just a small ranch.

Harris drove past a white two-story farmhouse and back to where a big barn and several large outbuildings stood. Several tractors were parked about, along with other pieces of equipment that she didn't recognize but could tell were for farming. Everything looked neat and orderly.

"Here we are," he said as he climbed out.

"This is a great place, Harris. Everything looks so well kept."

He smiled proudly. "Thanks, I do my best. Now, let's see how your pony is at unloading."

"Do you want me to help?"

"No, why don't you let me get it."

"Okay." She nodded and stepped back, controlling the urge to participate. She felt very protective of her horse, but reminded herself that it was Harris's trailer. She watched as Harris untied the lead and tried to get Bailey to back out.

Unfortunately, Bailey was better at getting in than getting out. It wasn't the first time she'd seen a horse do this, and she really wanted to give it a try herself but, at the same time, didn't want to intrude. Finally, she could tell Harris was getting frustrated, and she could stand by no longer.

"Why don't you let me give it a try?" she suggested.

"You think you can get him out?"

"Maybe."

Harris laughed. "Be my guest."

Jayne climbed into the trailer and spoke softly into Bailey's ear. Within seconds, the horse was backing up.

Harris made a noise that sounded like "Hmmph!" then slammed the trailer door shut and climbed into his pickup. She watched as he towed the trailer around, expertly backing it up and parking it neatly next to an outbuilding. That was something she couldn't do; every time she'd tried to back up a trailer she had jackknifed. While she waited, she walked Bailey around, talking to him about his new home and explaining how she would come to visit him every day after school.

"I'll show you where he'll be staying," said Harris. "It's the pasture in front, the one that parallels the road. You can park over there and get right to him without coming down the drive."

"Great," said Jayne, wondering if that was Harris's way of telling her to keep out of his way. She wouldn't be surprised after how she had harassed him on the way over. He probably thought she was a royal pain in the behind.

They turned Bailey loose in the pasture with a couple other horses, and he seemed right at home. Jayne looked at the water trough, checked the security of the gates, and surveyed the fence. Everything seemed to be in good shape. She realized she was fortunate to have found such a good place on such short notice. She shot up a silent thank-you to God, then turned to

Harris. "Thanks for letting me keep him here. I'm sure I'll sleep better knowing he's in such a good place." The other horses came over and began sniffing Bailey. One horse made a loud snorting sound and threw his head up as if he weren't sure he wanted to share his pasture with a newcomer. Jayne wondered if horses cared about bloodlines. Could they tell that Bailey was a half-breed, too?

"Horses are social animals," said Harris. "They might not get along at first, but I think in time they'll be okay. These two geldings are both boarders. I'll keep an eye on them for you."

"Hopefully they'll all become good buddies," said Jayne with a little uncertainty. She thought this must be the way moms felt when they left their children on the first day of school. She stroked Bailey's nose. "I'll be back to see you every day. I promise."

They went back to the barn, where Jayne gave Harris her work and home phone numbers in case of emergencies. They settled on monthly boarding rates and what was and was not covered in this arrangement. Part of her worried about this extra expense; she knew that horses were not kept cheaply. But then there was the money that Derrick had given her, and she could always take on a part-time job. The bottom line was she didn't care what it took—she *would* manage to afford it.

When she was ready to leave, Jayne used the barn phone to call Katherine. After she hung up, she looked around to see if Harris was nearby but couldn't spot him. Not knowing what else to do, she headed down the long driveway, hoping to meet Katherine as she came in. Jayne had suggested she just walk back to Katherine's to pick up her car, but Katherine convinced her that it was a lot farther than it looked; and besides, she wanted to have another look at Jayne's new horse.

As Jayne walked, she glanced around, trying to see where

Harris had disappeared to. He was definitely a different kind of guy. At least different from the kind she'd met in the city. He was polite and friendly, but not overly so. Although he might be considered a redneck in some circles, he didn't seem uneducated, and he certainly didn't lack confidence. He was probably just a typical Eastern Oregon cowboy, perhaps not all that different from Derrick, even though Derrick had tried to create the persona of a nineties kind of guy.

Harris was probably more the macho type, the kind of man who needed to have a submissive woman around, a cute little thing with a smile on her face and dinner on the table. Perhaps he already had one. And even if he didn't, Jayne was certainly not the type to fit into those shoes, or boots, or whatever. As if it mattered. Why was she even wasting her time thinking about such nonsense? It had been only a week since she'd ended one relationship; why would she think about another? Not that she was thinking seriously about it. She just wondered what kind of a man he was. Hopefully he was a reliable kind, one who could maintain a good, safe environment for her horse to stay. That was all she wanted.

She looked across the pasture to where Bailey was standing, grazing by himself in a corner near a clump of old locust trees. He was such a beautiful horse—everything she had always dreamed of. She admired his sleek, cocoa-colored coat and almost black mane. In fact, she thought his mane was about the same color as her hair. A warm rush filled her again. Bailey was her horse! After all these years, she had her very own horse. What more could she want? Suddenly she felt like dancing and singing and laughing all at once. She wished she could camp out in the pasture with Bailey all night long. Maybe she would sometime. Of course, Harris would probably think she was a little strange. Well, maybe she was.

SIX

◆

H e's a beauty," said Katherine as they sat in her parked
car next to the pasture where Bailey was grazing
peacefully. "I'm happy for you, Jayne. Sorry if I didn't
sound too enthused earlier. That was just the practical 'mom'
side of me talking. I know how spendy horses can be, and I
know you've mentioned that you're a little strapped for money
right now. But if God wants you to have this horse, he will
make a way for you. Right?"

"I really do believe that," said Jayne. "And I don't mind if I
need to get another job. It'll be worth it. Speaking of finances,
it just occurred to me that I didn't pay Harris for his time or gas
for picking up Bailey and bringing him here. What should I
do? How much do you think I should pay him?"

"Knowing Harris, I don't think he'll take it. He probably
considers it a good deed—just being neighborly, you know."

"But I'm not even his neighbor."

"That's all right. I am. And if it's really bothering you, maybe
you could do something special for him."

"That's probably a good idea, though I don't know what. I
don't think he really wants to see me around. I think I kind of
irritated him. I'm sure I talked way too much on the ride, but I
was still pretty excited about winning Bailey."

Katherine laughed. "Yeah, Harris isn't a real big talker. You
might have overwhelmed him a little."

Jayne shook her head. "Well, I would like to repay him. I'm
not exactly sure how, but if you think of anything, let me know."

Katherine agreed, then started the car engine. "Autumn and I are going to throw some burgers on the grill. Want to join us? It can be a celebration dinner."

"That sounds great, but can I run to the store and get something?"

"No, we've got what we need. And I don't know about you, but I'm starved."

"I guess winning Bailey has taken my mind off things like food. I still feel like I'm floating on a cloud."

"Almost as good as being in love?"

"Much better," said Jayne with a sigh. "I was never this happy with Derrick."

Katherine threw her head back and laughed as she pulled her little car out and headed for the next driveway.

When they reached the house, Autumn had already made a good start on dinner. Jayne and Katherine washed up, and before long, the burgers were done.

"It's so nice out here," said Jayne as she finished her last bite. She leaned back and looked across the horizon to where the sky was turning pink. "And I didn't think I was hungry, but those burgers were delicious."

"I buy my beef from Harris," said Katherine. "It's usually really good."

Jayne wondered if she'd ever be able to afford such a luxury. All her extra pennies would need to go toward grain and hay and possibly vet bills from now on.

"When are you going to ride Bailey?" asked Autumn.

"Mr. Bender said that Bailey was just getting saddle broken, but he still needs a lot of work. I can't wait to start working with him."

"Do you have a saddle and tack?" asked Autumn.

Jayne laughed. "Well, actually, I do. But it might be a problem out here in cowboy country. All I have is English."

"Go for it," said Katherine. "It's about time somebody expanded some of the narrow thinking out here in cowboy land. There's more than one way to ride a horse. Many Native Americans don't like saddles at all. They just throw a blanket on. Personally, I've gotten used to a saddle, but I enjoy a bareback ride from time to time."

Jayne knew she couldn't afford to buy a new saddle and would have to use her English one, so it was good to hear Katherine's words of encouragement. "Hey, I just remembered, I have something for you in my car," said Jayne as they cleared the picnic table. She deposited some dishes in the sink and ran to get the quilt.

She handed it to Katherine with a smile. "I hope you like it."

"This is beautiful, Jayne. The colors are perfect for my house. Where in the world did you find it? Certainly not in Paradise!"

Jayne smiled. "Actually, I made it a couple of years ago. When I saw your house, I thought it would be perfect. It's sort of a thank-you gift for being a good friend—right when I really needed a good friend."

Katherine hugged her. "I'll always treasure it. Thank you. It will remind me of our friendship." She carefully examined the quilt. "This is beautifully made, Jayne. You could easily sell something like this." She paused, then looked at Jayne closely. "You mentioned a part-time job earlier. I've been thinking about renting a space in the crafter's mall to sell my pottery, but I don't know if I'll have enough to fill a stall. Would you like to make some small quilts to go in it? We could go in together and split the rent. I bet if you had some ready by Thanksgiving we could do pretty well during the Christmas season."

"Katherine, I'd love to. In fact, I have a box full of quilted items that I could sell right now."

"Really? Well, I'll see about setting it up. I've got a fair amount of pottery that I'd like to get rid of. I had really wanted to put it in before rodeo time, but I got so busy getting ready for school. The lady who runs the mall offered me a stall at half price for the first month to try it out. If it doesn't pay off, we don't have to keep it up."

"This sounds like fun, Katherine. I sure hope it pays off. It would be a great way to make some extra money. And I'd still have plenty of time to spend with Bailey."

On Sunday morning, Jayne called her parents. She breezily explained about the breakup without going into the details, and before her mother could react, Jayne told her about winning Bailey.

"How in the world can you support a horse on half-time salary? And why do you want to stay in a strange town if you're not getting married?"

"Mother, I'm happy. I've never been so happy. I'm trusting God to take care of me. And so far, I'm fine."

"But it's only been a week—"

"I'm going to be fine, Mom. Really. Don't worry. I'll send some photos of Bailey. He's so beautiful. My new friend, Katherine, and I are going to sell quilts and pottery at the crafter's mall—"

"Quilts and pottery?" Her mother sounded aghast. "What about your job?"

"I'll still be teaching. I love teaching. Everything is great, Mom. Really. I have to go now. I'll write. Tell Dad I'm fine. And don't worry. Good-bye." Jayne hung up and caught her breath. She hadn't expected it to be easy, and yet it really hadn't been so bad.

She leaned back against a stack of boxes and looked at her cluttered living room. It was the second Sunday in a row that she hadn't gone to church. She didn't know where to go. Since she'd come to Paradise she had gone with Derrick and his family, and although she had made a couple of casual friends, she had no desire to go there now. That church had seemed a little too stuffy for her. She wanted to go to a church where the people felt real. Today she would worship God in the pasture with Bailey. She would have her own personal praise and thanksgiving service under the big blue sky.

She looked at all the unpacked boxes. Her apartment still looked like a miniature warehouse. Did she have anything here she could give to Harris to show her appreciation? She could bake something, but that would entail a trip to the store. Of course, he had made a long trip for her. Everyone had always liked her chocolate-chip cookies; maybe she could make a batch and take them with a thank-you card. She still didn't know if he had a wife or children, but if he did, cookies were something they would enjoy, too.

It was almost noon by the time she'd baked and boxed up the cookies and was on her way. She'd gathered a basket of brushes, a hoof pick, fly spray, and other horse-grooming products, and loaded them along with her tack and saddle into the back of her car. She wasn't sure how far she would get with Bailey today, but she figured it wouldn't hurt to have the saddle along just in case.

She had taken extra care in getting ready this morning. She knew it was silly since by the end of the day she would be dusty and sweaty, but she had put on a clean white shirt and silver earrings, French-braided her hair, and even applied a little blush and lip color. She wondered if Harris and his family, if he had a family, would be at church. She almost hoped that would be the case. Then she could just drop off the cookies on the porch and be out of their way. She really wasn't eager to meet his wife—if there was one.

She drove slowly down the road that ran next to Bailey's pasture. She spotted him standing in the sunshine. He was munching on a clump of grass. He looked just fine. She hoped that he was happy, that he liked his new home. She couldn't wait to see him up close again. But first things first. She needed, if only for Bailey's sake, to show her appreciation to Harris.

She parked in front of the house and turned off her car. It didn't look as if anyone were home. She studied the two-story clapboard house. It was neat but plain. No flowers in the beds, no touches of color. Other than an old wagon wheel and a leather horse yoke, there were no traces of personality on the wide front porch. The two upstairs dormer windows reminded her of the ones at Katherine's. But unlike Katherine's home, this house felt stark and almost sterile in its neatness. And with no one around it seemed deserted and sort of lonely. As soon as Jayne climbed from the car, a black-and-white Border collie began to bark and run toward her.

"Hi there," said Jayne, hoping to sound friendly. "I've come bringing gifts. Anyone home?"

The dog sniffed her leg and then wagged its tail, so Jayne could see there was no danger. But now it wouldn't be so simple just to leave the cookies unattended on the porch. Already the dog was stretching up with canine interest to smell the box. Having gotten this far, Jayne decided she should at least ring the doorbell. Then if no one was home she could drop the cookies off later. But as she stepped up to the door, she suddenly felt foolish and even a little intrusive. She really didn't want to irritate Harris anymore. She just wanted to say thanks and then to stay out of his way.

"Hello," said an older man from behind the screen door. "What can I do for you?"

"Hi, I'm Jayne. I, uh, I just wanted to thank Harris for helping me get my horse here yesterday, and so I baked him some cookies. I would have left them on the porch, but I was afraid the dog might enjoy them."

The man laughed and opened the screen door. "You're probably right about that. Cowboy does have a penchant for sweets. Come on in, Jayne. Harris told me all about the gal who won the horse. Congratulations."

Jayne stepped into the shadowy house. She wanted to hand the cookies to the man and make her departure, but since he was walking with a cane, she looked around for a place to set them down. "I don't mean to intrude—"

"It's no intrusion. Come on into the kitchen, Jayne. Set the box on the table. It's not often I get visitors. I guess I should introduce myself. I'm Jack McAllister, Harris's dad. I'm not good for much anymore with my bum leg and all, but I do make a mean pot of coffee. Care for some? I just made some fresh."

"That sounds good. Can I help you?"

"Nah, you go ahead and sit. I can get it."

Jayne sat down at a plastic-topped aluminum table with matching vinyl-covered chairs. The wallpaper in the kitchen was old and faded, with what were probably once red apples now turned a pinkish shade. She guessed the decor was circa 1960. Even the cup that Jack set before her looked like one she had seen at her grandmother's house.

"I think I ought to give these cookies a try before Harris gets home." Jack looked at her and his faded blue eyes twinkled, the same way she had seen Harris's do.

"Of course, by all means." She scooted the box over and smiled. "I guess Harris wouldn't mind if I had one too."

"Not at all." Jack took a bite, then smacked his lips. "These are good cookies, Janie. And the chocolate's still soft from the oven. You don't mind if I call you Janie, do you?"

Jayne had never really liked the name Janie before, but somehow, coming from this sweet old man, it sounded just fine. "Sure, you can call me Janie."

"Harris is at church. He doesn't go every Sunday, but some friends of his were getting their baby christened. I would have gone, but my arthritis was bothering me something fierce this morning. I'm feeling a little better now. It always helps to have pleasant company. So, Janie, how's that horse of yours?"

"He's wonderful." She hoped her voice didn't sound too dreamy.

Jack chuckled. "Harris says he has a little Arab blood in him. That don't bother you at all?"

"Not a bit. But I wish it didn't bother other people. Harris says that folks might give him a bad time for boarding a half-breed—"

"He said that?" Jack threw his head back and hooted. "Well, I wouldn't let it trouble you none. Harris is a big boy. He can take whatever they dish out."

Jayne sighed, relieved that at least Harris's dad wasn't concerned about Bailey being on their property. She liked Jack already. He seemed down-to-earth, without any sense of pretension. Nothing like Derrick's family.

"So what brings you to our neck of the woods? Harris said you weren't from around these parts."

"Well…" Jayne began instinctively to tell him the whole

68

story, then stopped herself. "I got a job teaching at the school."

"You came all the way out here just to teach school." His face told her that he wasn't buying her story.

"Well, yes—actually, the truth is I was engaged. It's no secret. I'm sure everyone in town knows about it."

"You that girl Derrick Long jilted to get back with Corky Galloway?"

Jayne felt her cheeks growing warm. "I'm surprised that it would get clear out here."

"Well, I do get to town once in a while. And I usually stop at the coffee shop to catch up on the latest. You were the talk of the town last week."

Jayne looked down at her half-filled cup of coffee and sighed. "I should have figured as much. I can't believe how everyone knows everyone's business around here. You'd think they'd have better things to do than talk about me. Hopefully it will blow over soon."

"Well, that depends on what the next juicy piece of gossip is. But usually these things only last a week or two. 'Course, your reputation is getting more interesting. Now you're not only the girl that Derrick jilted, but you're the girl who won a half-breed horse and decided to keep it."

"You might as well throw in that I ride English, too."

Jack let out a low whistle. "Well now, Janie, that might keep 'em talking for another two weeks."

Jayne groaned. Jack laughed. "But don't worry your pretty head. Just like the chaff disappears in the wind after a harvest, their words will all blow away before you know it."

She looked at him and smiled. "Thanks. I hope you're right." She finished up her coffee, then carried the cup to the sink and rinsed it out. "Thanks for the coffee, Jack. It's been a pleasure meeting you. I hope that you and Harris, and—uh—I don't know if there are others in your family, but anyway, enjoy the cookies."

"Just me and Harris live here. My wife died about twenty-five years ago, God rest her soul. She was a good woman. Harris was just a boy at the time. It's been me and him ever since. Two lonely old bachelors." Jack looked at her as if measuring her up, and the way he said the last line made Jayne think he was leading into something. But fortunately he stopped. She was sure her cheeks were glowing, and she wanted to get out into the fresh air and see Bailey.

"Thanks again, Jack. I'm going to check on Bailey now. I still can't believe I actually own a horse. I feel as though I'm having this wonderful dream and I don't want to wake up."

Jack laughed again. "Well, for a girl who just got jilted by the richest bachelor in town, you sure don't seem too broken up."

Jayne looked Jack in the eye and spoke in a low voice, but with a sly smile. "Well, don't you tell anyone this, but now that I have my own horse, I don't need a man."

She could still hear Jack hooting with laughter as she waved from her car and headed back down the driveway. She parked next to the road, climbed out, and called to Bailey. He lifted his head and began ambling over. She reached into her pocket and pulled out a carrot, which she began breaking into bite-sized pieces. At the grocery store this morning, she had purchased a large bag of carrots, enough to last a week or two, she hoped.

"Hi, sweet thing," she cooed as he came up and nuzzled his mouth into her hand. He eagerly munched down the piece of carrot as she stroked his soft nose. "You are so beautiful. We are going to have such fun." She fed him the rest of the carrot, then slipped the halter over his head, gently bringing the strap around and behind his ears to the buckle, talking softly the whole time.

Bailey continued munching without even a flinch as she

adjusted the leather straps. Then she took the lead and began to walk him around the pasture. The other two horses came up and looked at them with curiosity. She pulled another carrot from her pocket and shared it with them, hoping for Bailey's sake to make friends. One of the horses gobbled up the carrot, then snorted and threw his head, as if saying he still didn't like Bailey. Jayne ignored the snub and turned her focus to Bailey.

"Don't worry about those stuck-up old quarter horses," she said as they walked around. "They're probably just jealous of you."

She tied Bailey to the fence post and went to get her basket of grooming equipment. After a thorough brushing, she proceeded to check his feet and then clean them without any resistance on his part.

"You are such a good boy," she told him as she set down his last hoof. "You're doing so well maybe we should try out a saddle on you." He blinked a dark eye at her as if in agreement. She hurried back to her car to fetch the saddle, thanking God for giving her such a sweet-tempered animal. When she returned, he looked at her with trusting eyes, and she held the saddle blanket in front of him, allowing him to inspect it. Then she gently laid it across his back. He didn't even flinch. She did the same with the saddle. In no time she was cinching the saddle securely in place. She was tempted to mount him, but didn't want to push things too fast. Instead, she snapped the lunge line onto the halter.

"Let's see if you know how to do circles, Bailey," she said as she led him out into the center of the pasture. Slowly, after a few lopsided circles and a little confusion, Bailey began to understand. It was plain to see that he had carried a saddle before, and he moved gracefully. He was smooth and quiet and seemed healthy and smart.

"Thank you, Lord. This is a miracle horse!"

After half an hour of work, Bailey was performing almost perfect circles, and he seemed to be enjoying himself. He was moving in a slow, even trot. His ears were forward, with a pleasant expression. He looked like he had the makings of a show horse, not that she had any intention of training him that way. But it was nice to see that he had that kind of potential.

Jayne noticed Harris's pickup pull into the driveway, but she purposely didn't look up. She kept her focus on Bailey, hoping that Harris would see that she could stay out of his way and mind her own business when she worked with her horse. She really didn't want to intrude into his life. It would be fine if they became casual friends, and fine if they didn't. He seemed like a nice guy, and he was certainly attractive enough, but she was sure that they were as different as night and day, as Arabians and quarter horses, as English and western. And Jayne still wasn't convinced that there wasn't something brewing between Katherine and Harris; she would happily steer clear of anything that might damage her precious friendship with Katherine and Autumn. Besides, she had Bailey. Loving and caring for him would keep her life full and complete.

SEVEN

♦

During the next week, Jayne spent every spare moment with Bailey. As she'd expected, he responded well to her English saddle. She wondered if he appreciated that it was lighter and more comfortable than a western saddle. When she finally mounted him, he remained calm and quiet, nickering softly as if asking for reassurance. She kept a soothing hand on his shoulder, speaking to him constantly. He responded well to her voice, and she could tell that he trusted her.

With this kind of attention, along with treats, it didn't take him long to learn her commands. She knew he respected her, and it was mutual. Bailey was a highly trainable horse. She thanked God again and again for blessing her with such a fine creature. Having worked with many other horses, some who were quite obstinate, she knew that Bailey had a rare and desirable temperament. The kind of horse that horse owners searched for.

On Saturday, Jayne and Katherine met at the crafter's mall to set up their booth. Katherine had explained that arranging the booth, stocking it, and pricing the items were their responsibility, but the owner of the mall took care of everything else. Jayne had been glad to get rid of the quilted reminders of her broken engagement. She wouldn't have minded throwing them away but preferred the possibility of earning hay and grain money for Bailey.

"I stuck a wooden bookshelf in the back of my car," said

Jayne as she set down her box. "I wasn't sure if you needed anything extra to put your pots on."

"That would be great," said Katherine. "I've got some wooden crates, too."

They worked all morning arranging the booth. Jayne hung a large Amish-design quilt against the back wall of the booth. It was the first full-sized quilt she had made—pre-Derrick and thus not for sale—and it made a striking backdrop for Katherine's pottery. She then punched holes in small brown cards and tied them with raffia to use as price tags. With careful calligraphy she wrote down the price on each one and pinned or tied them to all the items. Katherine had brought some dried wheat and grasses that they arranged in the pots.

"This is looking pretty good, Katherine," said Jayne as she plumped several patchwork pillows and artfully arranged them in a corner.

Katherine nodded. "The combination of pottery and quilts makes for a nice display."

Customers were beginning to come into the mall, and Katherine and Jayne worked quickly to finish their booth. "I'll take these boxes and things back to the car," said Katherine, "while you finish putting those price tags on."

"Sounds good." Jayne continued working without looking up.

"Wow, look at these pillows," said a female voice from behind her. "Aren't they just to die for?"

"Let's go," said a hushed male voice that sounded familiar. Too familiar. Jayne froze. She knew it was Derrick. She remained bent over the tags as if she were concentrating on writing, but her hands were shaking and her stomach felt sick. If only they would just quickly move on.

"Wait a minute, Derrick. I want to look at this booth. It has some really neat stuff. Come back here." The woman's voice, and Jayne assumed it belonged to Corky, had a high-pitched, nasal sound to it. Part of Jayne longed to turn and stare, but the rest of her was afraid to see Derrick face-to-face. During the past week, with the excitement of her new horse, Derrick had seemed to turn into a foggy memory—almost like something that had never happened. She wanted him to stay that way.

"Excuse me, miss," said the woman. "Some items don't seem to be marked. Do you know how much these are?"

Jayne took a deep breath, straightened her back, and squared her shoulders. Might as well get it over with. This was a small town, and she wouldn't be able to avoid them forever. She shot up a silent prayer and turned, trying to curve her lips into what might pass for a casual smile.

"Can I help you?" she asked, keeping her eyes on the woman's face. It definitely was Corky; she recognized her from Katherine's yearbook. Only now her red hair was cut short and styled with plenty of hair spray. A thirty-mile-per-hour wind wouldn't undo that do. She looked as though she had lost weight since her high-school days, but her figure still filled out her tight teal Wranglers and matching western shirt. On her belt was an enormous silver rodeo buckle that looked as if it would cause serious injury if she tried to sit down.

Derrick was standing right behind her. "Uh, hello, Jayne," he said politely. "I guess I should introduce you."

Even under the makeup, Jayne could see the color drain from Corky's face. Corky turned to face Derrick. "This is her?" she whispered. He nodded.

"Hello, Derrick," said Jayne, unable to keep the coldness out of her voice. In that moment, she felt as though she hated him.

"I'm sorry to meet you like this—"

"Why be sorry, Derrick? It was bound to happen sooner or

later. Might as well get it over with." She stuck out her hand toward Corky. "Hi, Corky. I'm Jayne—Derrick's ex-fiancée. I'm sure you've heard all about me."

Corky took her hand and smiled weakly. "Hi, Jayne. I hope we won't be enemies."

Jayne forced a laugh. "Of course not. In fact, I should thank you."

Corky's eyes grew wide. "Thank me?"

"Yes, thank you for saving me from what would have been the biggest mistake of my life." Jayne smiled again and this time it was almost sincere. "Really, I wish you both the best. And just for the record, I'm very happy now. In fact, last week was probably the happiest week of my life." She looked directly at Derrick. "Did you hear that I won a horse?"

He shook his head blankly. It was clear that her take-charge attitude had caught him totally off guard.

"Well, I did. And he's absolutely wonderful. The love of my life." She knew her voice had increased in volume and intensity, but it was as if she couldn't stop. Her only alternative would have been to break down, and she couldn't do that. So she continued, speaking rapidly. "You know how I've always loved horses, Derrick. So much that I would have done almost anything to have one of my own. Well, now I do. And I couldn't be happier. I guess I should thank you too, Derrick. If you hadn't brought me here, I never would have won Bailey. In fact, I'm so thankful to both of you that I want to give you these."

She grabbed the two patchwork place mats Corky had been admiring and shoved them toward her. "Please, take these— with my blessings." Then Jayne turned on her heel and walked quickly away. She knew she'd behaved badly, but how was one supposed to react in a situation like that? She hoped that would be the worst of it. The ice had been broken, so perhaps they could all go on about their business in peace.

She ran into Katherine in the hallway by the bathroom and suddenly burst into tears.

"Jayne, what in the world happened?" asked Katherine as she escorted her into the rest room. "What's wrong?"

"Nothing really," said Jayne between sobs. "I'm really not sad. Just upset is all. But at least it's over."

"Did you see Derrick?"

Jayne nodded. "With Corky."

"Are you okay?"

Jayne blew her nose. "Yes. I probably said some unnecessary things. But I was so flustered. I knew this would happen someday, but it just took me by surprise." Jayne looked at Katherine and suddenly started to giggle a little. "I think I may have taken them by surprise, too. You should have seen their faces. I actually thanked Corky for saving me from the mistake of my life."

"You didn't."

"I did. And I thanked Derrick for bringing me here so I could find the real love of my life—" she exploded with laughter—"a horse!"

Now they were both laughing so hard that tears were running down their cheeks. Another woman started to come into the rest room but quickly backed up, shaking her head as if she had accidentally entered the loony bin. Finally, they calmed down long enough to dry their eyes and wipe their noses, and they sheepishly exited the rest room.

"I threw away some profits," said Jayne as they walked to the parking lot.

"How's that?"

"I gave them some place mats."

"Good for you, Jayne. I'd say that's sort of like turning the other cheek."

"I hope so. For a few seconds, I felt like I hated Derrick. It was an awful feeling. I don't want to hate anyone. I think it was my pride that was hating him. Seeing him reminded me of all the humiliation I felt when his mother told me the news, and it all seemed to bubble to the surface. I really wanted to hurt him."

"I'm sure that was a very normal feeling under the circumstances. I've felt that way before. But I know part of the reason that God doesn't want us to feel that way is because it's as harmful to us as it is to those we hate."

"You're right about that. Life's too short to waste on such destructive emotions." Jayne sighed as they stopped by her car.

"Are you going to be okay now?"

"Of course. Thanks for being there again, Katherine."

Jayne spent the rest of the afternoon working with Bailey. Just as she was about to call it a day, Harris came out and leaned against the fence. He didn't say anything, so she kept on riding. She could feel his eyes on her, watching quietly, as she rode along the fence in the pasture. She was proud of the way Bailey was responding and hoped that Harris would notice how well she handled a horse. Finally, she guided Bailey over to where Harris was standing and gracefully dismounted.

"He's really taken to the saddle," said Jayne as she unsnapped the chin strap on her riding helmet and slipped it off.

A slight frown crept across Harris's face. "You call that little slip of leather a saddle?"

Jayne looked at the sleek English saddle. It had taken her a year to save up for it in high school. "You might be surprised at how nice it is to ride English. You can get a good feel for the horse beneath you. Maybe you should try it sometime."

He laughed. "And maybe pigs can fly."

"You cowboys sure have a lot of pride."

Harris stuck his chin out and nodded. "That's right, we do. And it's not easy being the only rancher in the county with a gal out here riding in her equestrian getup with an English saddle, and on an A-rab to boot." He wore a half smile, but she could see there was more than a grain of truth behind his overly dramatic statement. She instantly felt defensive but didn't want to put him off. After all, she was thankful to have such a nice place to keep Bailey.

"I can see that my riding attire and saddle make you uncomfortable," she began cautiously. "Is this going to be a problem for you? I really don't want to cause you any trouble."

His bright blues eyes narrowed slightly, but not in a mean way. "Nah. I guess I can hold my own with anyone who wants to make an issue of it." He looked down at the riding helmet in her hand and shook his head. "But I just don't understand why you need this weird outfit to ride a horse."

She held up the dark brown velvet-covered helmet. "Well, when I took equestrian lessons, it was required that everyone wear helmets for safety reasons. And it's become a habit with me. I just feel safer. Do you want me to fall off my horse and get a concussion?"

Harris looked down at the ground. "No, of course not."

Jayne continued. "And jodhpurs are extremely comfortable." She pointed to her pants. "See, the roominess makes it easier to flex your thigh muscles when you ride, and the narrow part at the bottom is to slide into the boots."

"Cowboys wear their pants outside their boots," said Harris. "Only greenhorns tuck them in."

"Why do you wear them outside?"

"To keep things from falling into my boots."

Jayne nodded, then flicked the top of her riding boot with her crop. "English boots are made to fit snugly so nothing can fall into them." Then she pointed to her short fleece vest. "And the vest isn't necessarily English. But it makes a lot of sense because it keeps my torso warm but leaves my arms free to move. So there you have it—English Riding Attire 101."

Harris made the noise that sounded like "harrumph" again. She was getting used to his little noises but hadn't decoded them to know what each one meant. "Well, if it suits you, I guess there's not much more to say," said Harris. "Except that old quote, 'When in Rome, do as the Romans do.'"

"There was a time when the Romans were throwing the Christians to the lions."

Harris rolled his eyes at her, then grinned. "You always got a comeback, Janie." He turned and walked away. Despite herself, she watched him go, wishing she didn't think he was so handsome. He had called her Janie. Then she turned back to Bailey, thankful for such a good distraction.

That night, she enjoyed a long, hot soak in the tub. She promised herself that after her bath, she would begin to unpack boxes and organize her apartment. So far the only thing that was partially sorted out was her bedroom, and that was because she needed her futon to sleep on and had to keep her clothes organized for work.

No sooner had she opened a box than she heard a knocking on the door. Who would be visiting after nine o'clock? Thinking it might be a neighbor in need, she opened the door and peeked out, keeping the safety chain latched.

"Jayne? It's me, Derrick. I want to talk to you."

Her heart slammed against her chest. She did not want to talk to him. "I don't think there's anything to talk about, Derrick." She tried to make her voice sound strong and final, hoping that he would go away.

"Jayne, we need to talk. I'm sorry about today. I want to apologize to you in person. Can't you give me that much?"

Reluctantly she opened the door. "Come in," she said, waving her arm toward the piles of boxes. "Make yourself at home." She sat down on one box and pointed to another. In the old days, she wouldn't have wanted Derrick to see her with wet hair and wearing sweats, but she no longer cared. He sat down and leaned forward, his elbows on his knees.

"Jayne, when I saw you today, I was so shocked. For the last three weeks I have been trying to work up the nerve to talk to you—"

Jayne interrupted and was pleased to hear how controlled her voice sounded. "Don't you think it's a little late for explanations? The whole town knows everything. I don't know what you could possibly say to me that will make any of this easier. And like I said today, I'm glad. I truly am, Derrick. Actually, I do have something to say to you. It's a confession of sorts. I want you to know that I am sorry. I didn't realize it while we were engaged, but now I think I was using you a little, and I want to apologize. Oh, I liked you and I thought we would have a good marriage, but I wonder if I would have said yes if you hadn't had horses."

Derrick looked stunned. "Are you serious?"

"Like I said, I didn't realize it before. And I am sorry. Let's just both be thankful that it's all over with now. We've both been spared."

Derrick acted as though he'd been slapped. "I can't believe it, Jayne. I thought we really had something special—"

"Derrick!" Jayne jumped up and looked down at him. "You are the one who broke it off, not me. I'm just trying to show you the bright side of all this. I should think you would be grateful."

He sighed. "When I saw you today, Jayne, all I could think of was how beautiful you are, and why did I ever let you go? I must've been crazy."

Jayne groaned. "Derrick, don't start this—"

"No, I mean it. I think when I saw Corky was available it just brought back old memories, but after spending the last few weeks with her, I realize she's not the same as you. I wish we'd never gotten back together."

"Derrick, don't! I think you should leave now. You need to think about what you're doing—not only to me, but to Corky." Jayne walked toward the door.

"Jayne, are you saying that it's really over between us?"

"It seems to me that's what you said when you went back to Corky. That's what your mother told me when you wouldn't tell me yourself. That's what your letter told me when you sent me a good-bye payment. I almost sent it back, then decided that under the circumstances, you probably owed me that much. Thank you for it, by the way." She walked over to the door and pulled it open.

"Jayne, I can't believe you. You wouldn't really turn me away, would you?" His voice was whiny, making him sound like a spoiled little rich boy.

"Derrick, I feel sorry for you. But I don't love you. We need to go our separate ways. It really is for the best. Maybe Corky isn't the girl for you, but neither am I. Today, when I thanked you for bringing me here, I meant it. If I hadn't come, I wouldn't have Bailey. He's the best thing that ever happened to me. I thank God every day for my horse. I wish you well, Derrick. I really do. But I will never be a part of your life."

He stood and stared at her, as if he couldn't believe what he was hearing. "Think about it, Jayne. Think about everything you're throwing away right now."

"I've already thought about it, Derrick. Good night."

She closed the door behind him and locked it. Her heart was pounding and her head was spinning. She couldn't believe what had just happened. "Thank you, Lord," she prayed aloud, "for getting me out of that relationship before it was too late." She remembered the Bible verse about all things working together for good for those who love God. In her case it was certainly true. She was not so sure about Derrick. She decided to pray for him—and for Corky, too.

Eight

The end of September was harvesttime in Paradise. Everywhere you looked, wheat fields were in various stages of harvest. Combines ran night and day, and large trucks full of wheat continually shuttled back and forth along the highway. Jayne had noticed how busy Harris was, and she'd heard little more than a "howdy" from him in the last few days. When she had mentioned the dark shadows under Harris's eyes to Jack, he had informed her that Harris was putting in up to twenty hours a day. It worried her, but it was none of her business.

However, when she noticed that Harris's focus on his harvest had distracted him from his livestock, she grew very concerned. Since she came every day to work with Bailey, she made sure that the water trough he shared with the other two boarded horses stayed full. But by the middle of the week, she noticed that both Harris's stallion and the six steers in the opposite pasture had completely run out of water. She filled both of these troughs, then decided to pay a visit to the barn where the mares were kept.

The barn had a corral attached to it that connected to yet another pasture. Normally Harris let the mares out into the corral, and often into the adjoining pasture, for exercise. But today they had not even been out of their stalls, and the water trough for the mare who was expecting a foal this winter was bone-dry. Jayne let the mares out and filled their water troughs. Then she marched out to the wheat field where Harris was working with the harvesters. How dare he treat animals, even his own animals, like this! It took her twenty minutes to get close to where they were working, and that was walking fast. Immediately the combine stopped, and Harris leaped down from the cab and ran toward her, his face full of concern. The driver of the other truck stuck his head out the window and watched with curiosity.

"What's wrong?" Harris shouted above the sound of the noisy machinery.

Suddenly Jayne felt more than a little foolish and quite conspicuous. It had seemed like such a big deal just minutes ago, but now she wasn't so sure. "I, uh, I—"

"What is it?" he asked, grabbing her by the arm. "Tell me. Is it Dad? Is he okay? What's wrong?"

"No, it's not your dad, Harris. It's your animals—"

"What is it? Did one of them get injured? Do you need to call a vet? The number is right next to the phone in the barn—"

"No, no one is hurt. But they were out of water—"

"What?" Harris stared at her as if she had two heads. "You came all the way out here just to tell me they were out of water?"

"No. I was mad—"

"You were mad because my animals were out of water?"

"Your mares hadn't been let out. Amber was completely out of water."

Harris took off his hat and scratched his head, still looking at her strangely. "I don't get it, Jayne. You came out here just to tell me that? Don't you know that you're wasting precious time out here? I have a crop to get in."

"Well, yes, but I was concerned—"

"Well, if you want to be concerned about something, be

concerned that you're interrupting my work."

"Sorry to have bothered you!" She turned on her heel and stormed off. She heard the engines rumble loudly as they returned to their *important* work. As if cutting grain were more vital than thirsty animals with no water to drink. She huffed all the way back to the barn. When she reached the corral, the two mares lifted their heads from the water trough as if to say thanks.

"You're welcome, ladies," she called out. "Sorry your master isn't more thoughtful."

"Hey, there, Janie!" She looked up to see Jack on the back porch, leaning on his cane and waving to her. "Come on over and have some lemonade," he called. The border collie ran up to her, barking and wagging his tail. She bent over and stroked his smooth head.

"Hi there, Cowboy," she said to the dog. Then she looked up at Jack. "That sounds good, Jack. I'll be there in a minute." She double-checked the gate to the corral, worried that she might have left it unlatched in her haste earlier. She didn't want to be guilty of animal neglect, especially after her confrontation with Harris.

"Saw you walking out to where they're working, Janie," said Jack as he handed her a tall glass of lemonade. The glass had a cartoon character on it and looked like something that was won at a county fair. She took a long sip and sighed.

"Yes, I had words with your son." She smiled. "Thanks for the drink, Jack. I needed this."

Jack chuckled. "'Had words with my son'? That sounds like trouble. Is my boy giving you a hard time?"

"No. But his animals were out of water and the mares hadn't been let out all day."

Jack pressed his lips together. "I sure wish I could get around better. The boy needs help, and this darn arthritis makes me feel useless."

"No, it's not your fault, Jack. And probably not Harris's, either. He's just too busy."

"This is a hard time of year."

Jayne nodded. "I know it is. I'm sorry I went out there now. I probably didn't help things a bit. But I was so irked about the animals that I just didn't think." She paused. "But I've got an idea. What if I help him out a little? I don't mind checking on the animals. I'm already out here every day anyway."

"That'd be just the ticket, Janie. In trade, we'll give you free pasture for your horse, maybe throw in some hay, too."

"Really? That would be nice. But what about Harris? Do you think he'll agree?"

"If I tell him to, he will." Jack winked. "This is still my farm. At least until I kick the bucket, which might not be too far off judging by the way I felt this morning."

"Oh, don't say that, Jack."

"Don't see as it should matter much. I'm pretty much good for nothing—"

"That's not true. You do the bookkeeping. You help keep up things around the house. You're good company for Harris. And you know everything there is to know about farming."

"Nah, not anymore. They're always coming up with some newfangled ways to do things. Harris passed me up long ago when he went to agricultural school."

"Even if that's the case, everything else I said is true, Jack. Harris needs you."

"Maybe so. Although sometimes I wonder if I wasn't around, maybe Harris would do something about getting himself a wife." He looked over at Jayne as if she were a likely candidate.

"Don't look at me, Jack," she said, holding her hands up. "I just got free of one bad relationship. I'm not looking for another."

"Who says it would have to be a bad one?"

Jayne laughed. "And what makes you think your son is looking for anything? Seems to me the man can take care of himself. And if he needed a wife, I'm sure he'd go right out and find himself one."

"Maybe. But I wouldn't be so sure."

"Why's that? Doesn't Harris like women?"

Jack laughed. "I reckon he likes them—at least from a distance."

"Has he had any relationships with women? Any girl-friends?"

"Not in the last few years."

"What about Katherine? He seems to like her."

Jack scratched his head as though considering this possibility. "You know, Janie, there was a time in my life when I would have taken exception to a comment like that. But I think I've gotten wiser in my old age."

"You mean because Katherine is Native American?"

"There's still a lot of folks around here that think that way, Janie. But I happen to think real highly of Katherine. And if it were the right thing, I wouldn't disapprove in the least."

"What do you mean by the right thing?"

"Well, I've seen them two together and they're good friends and all, but I just don't see any spark."

"Spark?"

"You know, what you kids call chemistry. I just don't think they've got it."

Jayne laughed. "I see. So do you think Harris has ever had that kind of spark for anyone?"

"Yes, I believe he did once. But it was a long time ago."

Jayne didn't want to pry, but she did feel curious. She helped herself to some more lemonade, then pretended to study the picture of Wiley Coyote on the glass.

"Harris had a girlfriend back when he was young," Jack continued. "He was a couple years older than her. I think he took her to his senior prom. Her name was Jill Emerson, and her folks owned a family restaurant downtown. Harris and Jill went out real regular for at least two years. I think everyone expected them to get married. Then just the week before Jill was to graduate, she and her dad were driving home after work one night—Jill helped her dad out part-time at the restaurant—and a drunk driver smashed into them head-on, going about ninety miles an hour. Jill was killed instantly. Her dad died the next day. Later that summer, Mrs. Emerson sold the restaurant and took the little brother to live in California. It was a real sad time for everyone."

"It must have been awful for Harris."

"It was. That was the year I talked him into going to the state college. He'd always been a real bright boy. I told him to take whatever classes he wanted. What I really hoped was that he'd find himself a gal to help him get over losing Jill."

"Did he?"

"Not that I ever heard of. He worked real hard taking agricultural science. Made me proud. Then he came back here to work the farm. A man couldn't ask for a better son."

Jayne nodded. "So do you think he ever got over her?"

"I'm not sure. He's had a few women friends over the years, but he never sticks with them long enough to get to know them. Sometimes I think he's afraid."

"Afraid?"

"Yeah. I think what with losing his mama and then losing Jill, he might worry that he'll just lose another. But that may just be an old man's silly imagination."

"Maybe not, Jack. Have you ever talked to Harris about this?"

"Don't know as I've ever talked to anyone about this, Janie. Men around these parts don't usually talk like this. I guess I must be getting old. Sometimes I remind myself of an old woman."

Jayne laughed. "I don't see how."

"Well, I'm just starting to see some things differently, I guess."

"Like you said, you're probably getting wiser in your old age."

"Well, old age ought to be good for something."

Jayne stood up and set her glass in the sink. "Thanks for the lemonade, Jack."

"Anytime, Janie. It's always a pleasure talking with you. I'll mention to Harris that you'll be looking after the critters, at least until harvest is finished."

"I appreciate it. Maybe you or Harris could make me a list for the livestock. Obviously I know about the water, but I'm not sure how much hay the steers get and whatnot."

"Sure, I'll have one for you tomorrow."

"Thanks, Jack." She bent down and patted Cowboy on the head. "You're a good dog, aren't you, boy?" Cowboy looked up at her with adoring eyes, and his tongue hung out the side of his mouth in a ridiculously charming way.

"Looks like he likes you, Janie," said Jack.

"I seem to get along better with animals than men—present company excluded, Jack."

Jack laughed. "That's okay. Sometimes I think I do, too."

She went back out to check on Bailey. She had already ridden him and taken him through his paces, but it was always so hard to leave him in the evening. He met her at the fence, gently nudging her shoulder with his nose. "Hi, sweet thing," she said as she climbed onto the top rail of the fence and sat down. He put his head down and chomped contentedly on the tall grass next to her.

She listened to the rhythmic sound of his munching and looked out at the sky, thinking about some of the things Jack had told her about Harris. Once again, she regretted that she'd gone out and made such a big deal about Harris's livestock. Like a video, she replayed the expression on his face as he leaped from the combine. He had looked so alarmed. He'd probably thought that she was going to tell him his father was hurt, or even dead. Poor Harris. She wondered if the loss of his mother and girlfriend had affected him as much as Jack seemed to think. She supposed it was possible. But what did all this have to do with her? As much as she liked Harris, they really had very little in common, and she didn't think he cared much for her. It seemed they were often at odds. And despite what Jack thought, Jayne wasn't entirely convinced that there was nothing between Harris and Katherine.

Suddenly Jayne remembered she had promised Katherine that she'd stop by after working with Bailey. The week was already half over, and she and Katherine had not shared more than two sentences. This week they were getting ready for open house at school, and they were both working fast and hard to make their classrooms as attractive as possible. On top of all that, Katherine had to take Autumn to the orthodontist yesterday.

Jayne hopped down from the fence and stroked Bailey's neck. "Good-bye, sweet thing," she said. "I'll see you tomorrow." She hopped in her car and drove to Katherine's. As soon as she climbed out of the car, Shamee came trotting up and greeted her with a wet kiss on the hand.

"Hi, Jayne," called Autumn from the porch. She was busily picking burrs out of a cat's furry coat.

"Who's this?" asked Jayne, leaning over to get a better look at the tiger-striped cat stretched out in Autumn's lap.

"This is Lazarus," said Autumn without looking up.

"Interesting name for a cat."

"Well, when I found him he was half dead. And remember how Jesus raised Lazarus from the dead?"

"Right," said Jayne. "I get it. That's a good name. So is your mom inside?"

"Uh-huh. Go on in, Jayne."

Jayne found Katherine sitting at her kitchen table surrounded by various sizes and shapes of clay pots. "Looks like you've been busy," said Jayne as she picked up a small pitcher with a nicely curved handle.

"Well, I stopped by the crafter's mall today, and you wouldn't believe how picked over our stall looks. Our stuff has been selling like hotcakes. You're going to need to get busy too. Most of your quilted items are gone, and the cashier told me that several people have tried to buy that big quilt you hung up for display."

"You're kidding!"

"Nope. We're the hottest stall in the crafter's mall." Katherine smiled proudly.

"This is great. Well, I've got some quilting projects that are almost done; I suppose I could finish them up."

"If you need money, it might be wise to strike while the iron's hot, as Jack would say."

"That's probably true. So, when have you had time to make all those pots?"

"I didn't make them. I bought them from my mom. She's

really a much better potter than I am, but she hates to apply the glaze. She says it's too hard on her eyes, and plus her hands are a little unsteady. And this is my favorite part, so we worked out a deal. This will come in handy now, especially since Autumn needs braces."

"I wonder if we made our prices too low," said Jayne as she sat down.

"That could be. Maybe we could experience a little inflation."

"You know what they say about supply and demand. Speaking of that, I just took another job of sorts. I told Jack that I'd help with the livestock care during harvest in exchange for pasture. That is, if Harris agrees. Although after what I did this afternoon, he'll probably evict both Bailey and me."

"What did you do?"

Jayne told Katherine about the confrontation, and Katherine just laughed. "Serves Harris right. He should know better. You can't neglect your animals like that."

"I agree. But after talking to Jack, I felt sort of bad."

"Why's that?" asked Katherine as she held up a pot to her nose and skillfully painted a thin line all the way around.

"Jack told me about how Harris's high-school sweetheart was killed. I felt so bad for Harris. I know it was a long time ago, but it's still so sad."

"Oh, yes. Sometimes I almost forget about that. Jill Emerson was just a couple years older than me. She was a sweet girl. I remember going into Emerson's restaurant, and Jill always treated me nicely. It was so sad when she and her dad were killed. For some of us, it was even more sad...."

"What do you mean?"

"The drunken driver was from the reservation." Katherine looked up with somber brown eyes. "Somehow, when something like that happens, it seems that all the people pay for it."

"That's not fair."

"Life's not fair, Jayne. And it was a bad summer that year." Katherine looked over her shoulder to the porch. "That was my wild year. The year I got into trouble."

Jayne nodded. "Well, you've certainly come out of it fine, Katherine."

"Thank God." Katherine set down the pot. "But why was Jack telling you about that?"

"I think he's worried about Harris. He's trying to figure out why he hasn't gotten married. How old is Harris, anyway?"

"About thirty, I think."

"Poor Jack. I think he was hoping to match me up with his son."

"Aha," said Katherine. "And how do you feel about that?"

"Actually, I told Jack that I thought you and Harris might have something going—"

Katherine burst out laughing. "You didn't! Why would you think such a thing?"

"Why not?"

"Well, Harris is nice enough. But I think of him more as a big brother. I couldn't imagine feeling romantic about him."

"Why not?"

"Because I don't. You just can't force some things."

Jayne smiled. "You're right. But I wanted to make sure. Just in case."

"Ahh, so you might be interested."

"I didn't say that."

"Okay. But maybe you're thinking about it, getting ready just in case something develops?"

"Maybe. But I doubt it. Most of all, I wanted to be sure that there was nothing going on between you two. I wouldn't want to hurt my best friend by getting in the middle of something."

"Well, I appreciate your asking. But, believe me, Jayne, Harris and I could only be friends."

"Is it because he's white?"

"No. I don't think that way."

"Sorry. I just wondered."

"It's all right. We're friends, Jayne. I want you to feel free to ask me whatever you want."

"Okay. Let me ask you this then…"

"What is it?"

"Do you have anything good to eat?"

Katherine threw her head back and laughed. "Jayne Morgan, you are like the sister I never had."

NINE

For the next few days, Jayne took care of the livestock. She was careful and conscientious and hoped that Harris approved, although she doubted that he even checked her work. Jack had given her a short list Harris had written that was very straightforward and helpful. At the bottom of the paper he'd written that he would trade next month's pasture fee in exchange for the livestock care she gave during harvest. It seemed more than fair, and Jayne did not want to let him down. She could tell that harvest would soon be over, but Jayne hoped she could continue to care for the animals.

One sunny afternoon, she saddled up Bailey and decided to enjoy the weather. No telling how many nice days would be left. There was definitely a trace of fall in the air, and she could smell smoke coming from a nearby farm. It was a pleasant aroma, reminding her of a bonfire. Life seemed pretty good right now.

Last night they had held open house at school, and the evening had gone well. It had been fun to meet all the parents. They were appreciative of the little program of songs and finger plays that she and the children had performed, and they seemed genuinely interested in what their children were learning. It had been a good feeling to know that her first year of teaching was off to a good start. Unfortunately, that pleasant feeling had been cut short when she encountered Derrick waiting by her car in the dark parking lot behind the grade school. She shook her head in disgust as she remembered his pleading voice, begging her to reconsider their relationship. She had been trying to put the whole thing out of her head, but it was so strange. Unnerving, actually. She never would have believed Derrick could act like this. Bailey swung his head around and gave her a quick look, as if he instinctively knew that something was troubling her.

"It's okay, Bailey," she said in a calming voice. "You're doing just fine, sweet thing." She nudged him with her knees and gave the command to trot. He fell into the rhythmic motion without hesitation. His trot was a little smoother than some horses she had ridden, but it was still a bit of a workout. She flexed her thigh muscles and steadied herself, keeping her back straight and knees slightly bent. Gripping with her knees, she posted up and down every other beat of the trot, allowing Bailey's movement to gently thrust her up off the saddle and then back again.

After about ten minutes of trotting, she squeezed him into a gentle canter and let him go the full length of the pasture. She allowed her muscles to relax a little but remained focused on maintaining correct posture. She loved the feel of the wind in her face and wished she could take Bailey for a long ride, but she didn't want to push him too fast. The warmth of the sun soaked through her jacket, and once again she marveled at how therapeutic riding felt.

"Hey, there."

Jayne looked over her shoulder to see Harris leaning against the fence on the west side. She slowed Bailey and walked over toward him.

"Hey, Harris. Looks like you've just about got your wheat beat." She nodded over to the wheat field, which was mostly reduced to golden stubble.

"Yep, Howard is finishing up right now." He took off his hat and waved it as if in celebration. "And then it's done."

"That must feel good." Jayne looked away. She hadn't apologized yet for interrupting his work the other day. She wasn't even sure that she should. After all, she had only been concerned about the livestock; she hadn't really meant to upset him.

"Is everything okay?" asked Harris.

"Yeah, sure, I guess so. Why do you ask?"

"I was watching you ride, and your expression looked a little funny. Like something was troubling you. Everything going all right?"

She slid off the saddle and studied Harris's face. She found it hard to believe that he could have read her expression so easily while she was riding. But he looked as if he were genuinely concerned. "Well, I guess I was worrying about something. But it was nothing much. And I was thinking about how therapeutic riding could be."

"Might even be cheaper than seeing a shrink. But sometimes it's nice to have someone to talk to. If you need a set of human ears, that is."

She tried not to look as amazed as she felt. This was a side of Harris she hadn't seen before. Maybe being done with harvest brought out the best in a man. "Well, I wouldn't want to burden you with my problems—"

"I wouldn't ask if I didn't want to hear. And by the way, I wanted to apologize."

"For what?"

"The other day, out in the field. I didn't mean to jump all over you. I guess when I saw you coming out all dressed up in your funny riding clothes, I thought something must've been really wrong to make you walk all the way out there."

"I wanted to apologize too. I just wasn't thinking clearly. I was so upset about your livestock that I forgot you were pretty consumed with getting your wheat in. I'm sorry."

"Well, I probably need to learn to think before I speak."

"You're not the only one." Jayne was now standing directly across from him, with the fence rail running between them. His eyes were clear and bright, and she couldn't help comparing them to the sky that was behind him. His eyes were definitely bluer.

"You've been doing a fine job taking care of the livestock."

"Thanks. I appreciate the deal we worked out."

"Would you be interested in doing it on a more regular basis? I mean, I don't want to impose on you, but Dad said that he thought you didn't mind...."

"Sure, I'd be glad to."

"When the weather gets colder I usually need to feed them twice a day, and I check their water for ice in the winter. I use automatic water thermostats that are supposed to keep them from freezing, but you can't always trust those. It'd be nice to have a little extra help, if you're sure you want to. It can be pretty rough when it gets cold. And I was meaning to ask—you had mentioned wanting a stall for Bailey?"

"I was hoping that I could." Jayne was also hoping it wouldn't be too expensive, but maybe helping with the live-stock would offset the extra expense.

"I think we can work it out." Harris smiled and stretched out his arms. "The wheat's in, and I feel like celebrating. I was planning on going out for a big steak dinner. Would you like to join me?"

Jayne looked down at her dusty riding clothes. "Well, yes, sure, I'd love to, but I'm not really dressed for—"

Harris laughed. "Nor am I. But I plan to shower and shave." He grinned up at her. "Actually, you don't look so bad. It'll probably take me a lot longer than you to clean up. How about if I pick you up at—" he glanced at his watch—"say seven-thirty?"

"That sounds great."

She gave him directions to her apartment, then hopped on Bailey and galloped over to her car, where she removed the saddle and bridle in record time and didn't even brush out Bailey's coat where the saddle blanket had matted it down slightly.

"Sorry, sweet thing," she said as she set the saddle in the backseat of her car. "I'll make up for that tomorrow morning. It's a good thing tomorrow's Saturday. We'll have the whole day together. But tonight, I have a date." She stroked his nose, then gave him a kiss. "But don't get jealous. I couldn't possibly love anyone more than you!"

She took the shortcut home and ran up the stairs, taking two at a time. Inside her apartment she groaned when she saw her still unpacked boxes. What would Harris think of her? Well, she didn't have to let him inside. Of course, that might seem even worse. She took a quick shower, then rummaged through her closet in search of the perfect outfit. After discarding several possibilities, she decided to go western, since Harris almost always had seen her wearing her English riding clothes.

She slipped on a denim skirt and a white Western shirt with pearl snaps and embroidery around the yoke. Then she pulled on her dark brown Roper boots and a matching belt with a silver buckle. It was what she called understated western, and it suited her just fine. She doubted that she'd ever wear fringed jackets or pointy-toed boots.

She brushed out her long hair, and for a change decided to let it fall loose down her back. She usually held it back in a barrette or in a thick braid, partly because it was easy and partly because it kept people from making a big deal about her hair.

She knew her hair was unusual because of its length—nearly to her waist—and its thickness. Sometimes she enjoyed the compliments, but usually they embarrassed her. Sometimes she wondered why she didn't just cut it altogether. But that Bible verse about a woman's hair being her glory seemed to stick with her, and she couldn't bring herself to have it cut. Maybe someday.

She studied her reflection critically in the full-length mirror. As usual, she looked long and narrow. Even her face seemed narrow, and the long, straight hair probably didn't help. But that was who she was, and there wasn't much she could do about it. She'd never been curvy, and didn't know if she ever would be. She dabbed on a little lipstick and blush, hoping that would help. Then she tried out some new silver earrings that she had gotten when she was still with Derrick but never worn. If she'd kept the receipt, she probably would have taken them back, but she was embarrassed to try to return them without it. Well, maybe it was time to enjoy them.

She stepped back and looked again. Better. Just then she heard a knock at the door, and her heart began to beat a little faster. But it was only Harris, she told herself; just the man who pastured her horse. Why should she get all excited?

"Hi," she said brightly as she opened the door. But it wasn't Harris. It was Derrick.

"Hi, Jayne." Derrick smiled. "You sure look nice."

"That's because I'm going out." Jayne looked over his shoulder to see if Harris was coming.

"Where are you going?"

"It's not really any of your business."

"Oh, I see. Is it a date?" The way he said it made it seem like something dirty.

"Derrick, like I said last night, we are over with. Period.

Nothing more to talk about. Go back to Corky."

Derrick laughed. "Are you sure we're over with, Jayne? Are you sure you can get rid of me that easily?"

"Seems to me that you were the one who did the getting rid of, remember?"

"Right. So now I have to win you back? Like the gallant knight—"

"No. That's ridiculous. I want you to leave me alone, Derrick. Okay? I don't want to be mean, but I have absolutely no interest in seeing you. As far as I'm concerned, we're finished. Please stop harassing me like this. It's really starting to bug me." Her voice had gotten loud, but she wanted him to get the message.

"Harassing you? You call a friendly little visit harassing?"

"This isn't a friendly visit. Now, I'm asking you nicely—please leave." She started to close the door, afraid he might stick his foot in to stop her, but thankfully he didn't.

She closed the door, turned the lock, then leaned against it. Why was he doing this? Was it just because he couldn't have her that suddenly he wanted her? She sighed deeply, then whispered, "Dear God, please show me what to do." A few moments later, another knock sounded on the door. She jerked the door open, unsure of what she would say, but this time it was Harris.

"Thank goodness!" she exclaimed.

"And to you too," he said with a curious smile. "What's up?"

"Oh, you probably don't want to hear about it. I'm just thankful you're here."

"Okay. Are you ready to go? I'm starved."

"Yes. I'm more than ready." She stepped out and smiled up at him. "Sorry, I just had an unwanted visitor, and I'm trying to get my bearings back together."

Harris looked down at her. "Looks like you've got them pretty well together to me."

"Thanks," she said. "I think."

They walked down the stairs and to his pickup. He opened the door, and she climbed in and watched as he walked around the front of the truck. He had on blue denim Wranglers and a black western shirt. His hat didn't look new, but it was clean and nicely shaped. The color was almost the same as Bailey's coat—a soft, deep brown.

"Well, I hope you're hungry," said Harris as he turned on the ignition.

"Actually, I am."

He turned and looked at her. "Looks like you could stand to put a little meat on your bones."

"You're one to talk, Slim."

He laughed. "Well, I didn't mean to insult you. But so many women are afraid to eat, or they eat like birds. I hope you're not like that."

She smiled. "Actually, I do eat like a bird.

Harris shook his head.

"Didn't you know that birds eat several times their body weight each day?"

"Plumb forgot!" Harris chuckled and put the truck into gear. "Yep, you've always got a comeback, Janie."

"Not always, but I've never been any good at holding my tongue."

"Well, at least you don't keep it all bottled up inside."

She wanted to ask him if he did, but decided, for a change, to keep quiet. No need to push things too fast. "So where are we going?"

"O'Malleys. I haven't been there for a while, but they have the best steaks in this part of the country. Ever been there?"

"Actually, I have." She had gone there a couple of times with Derrick, but she didn't want to be reminded of that right now.

"Ahh, there's that look again, Jayne. Is something troubling you?"

"Well, if you really want to know, it's not some*thing*, but some*one*."

"Derrick?"

"How did you know?"

"It's a small town."

"But you've been so busy with harvest—"

"The guys like to chat when we take breaks."

Jayne nodded. "You mean gossip."

Harris smiled. "Call it what you like. But I did pick up on the fact that you used to be engaged to Derrick Long, heir to the Long throne, and he broke it off with you to take up with his old sweetheart, Corky Galloway."

Jayne laughed. "That's a pretty good start. Is that *all* you know?"

"You mean there's more?"

"Unfortunately. But I guess I should be thankful that you didn't already hear it. Maybe it hasn't made it to the jungle drums yet."

Harris frowned. "What, has Derrick changed his mind again?"

Jayne nodded. "That's what he says."

"Meaning you don't believe him?"

"Oh, I don't know what to believe. I don't even care. I just wish he would leave me alone. I keep telling him we're through, but he just doesn't take me seriously. I don't know what his problem is."

"His problem is he's spoiled and used to getting what he wants."

"Well, he won't this time." She stuck her chin out for added emphasis, then glanced over at Harris out of the corner of her eye. She saw him smile.

Harris pulled into the parking lot of the restaurant. It looked pretty busy, but when they walked in, he spoke briefly to the hostess and they were seated within minutes.

"How did you swing that?" she asked as they were seated at a table by a window that looked out over rolling plains.

"Ever hear of reservations?"

"But wasn't it sort of late to get them?"

"Nah, I called earlier this afternoon."

"So were you coming alone, or did someone else stand you up?"

He grinned sheepishly. "I made reservations for two. I was feeling hopeful that you would be up for a night out."

She smiled and unfolded her napkin. "Sorry, I didn't mean to grill you like that. I guess I'm still feeling a little edgy."

"I noticed a pickup leaving your apartment complex when I arrived. Had Derrick been by your place?"

She told him how Derrick had caught her by surprise after the open house last night, then once again tonight. "It's more than irritating. It's weird. I almost feel like I'm being stalked or something. I know that's silly, but he just keeps popping up, and I'm not sure how to handle it."

"Well, it's a tough one. The Longs have a lot of influence in this town. As irritating as Derrick is, you really don't want to make him or his family your enemy if you can help it. But on the other hand, it's wrong for him to keep bugging you like that. Are you sure you made it clear that it's over between the two of you?"

"Crystal clear."

Harris scratched his chin. "Maybe next time, if there is a

next time, you could tell him that you'll tell Corky if he keeps after you."

"What good will that do?"

"Well, as far as I know he hasn't broken it off with Corky. At least I haven't heard about it. It might be that he's keeping her in the stands in case he can't get you back, and if that's the case, he won't want to mess things up with her. Especially seeing how fond his family is of her. He might not want to burn that bridge yet."

"I think you might be on to something. Thanks."

They ate porterhouse steaks together and laughed and joked, and Jayne felt as if she had known Harris for years. She wondered about what Jack had said, but perhaps he was wrong. Maybe Harris had just been too busy to have a relationship with a woman. Or maybe it was just that the right woman hadn't come along yet.

TEN

◆

After what proved to be an unexpectedly wonderful night out with Harris, Jayne hoped that they might do something together again in the near future. But the next week passed without more than a few words between them. Harris was polite but at the same time somewhat distant. Aloof.

The week passed quietly in other ways, too. Derrick made no more surprise appearances at her door, and Jayne thought that perhaps he had finally taken the hint, but if not, she was prepared to bring Corky into it just as Harris had suggested. She continued to care for Harris's livestock after school each day along with working with Bailey. It seemed she was spending every spare moment out on the ranch, but she didn't mind. It was where she wanted to be. She loved the smell of the hay, the earth, the animals. She knew them all by name now, and they knew her and were always glad to see her coming. There was something comfortable and comforting about children and animals. Sometimes she thought she would be content if that was all her life consisted of.

The weather grew progressively cooler, and the sun set a little earlier each evening. It was the perfect time of year for riding, and Bailey was becoming more ridable each day. Friday was a noncontract day, so there was no school, and Jayne, Katherine, and Autumn celebrated by saddling up their horses and riding over to where Katherine's mother, Joanne, lived. Her home was on the reservation too, but it took about an hour to get there on horseback. It was a fun ride, and Jayne enjoyed seeing some of the more remote parts of the reservation. It surprised her that some people weren't more friendly to Katherine and Autumn, but then maybe that was just their way.

Joanne's house wasn't much more than a shanty, but it was filled with her beautiful pottery and intricate beadwork. All the surfaces were coated with a fine, reddish terra-cotta dust, but Joanne didn't even seem to notice. She just puttered about, moving between the brick-and-board shelves that were crowded with all sizes and shapes of pots. In fact, Joanne reminded Jayne of a pot. She was short and round, and her skin was a light shade of terra-cotta.

It was rather fascinating being in Joanne's home, almost like being in another country. Jayne felt somewhat like an intruder. It was clearly another culture, and while Joanne treated her politely enough, she felt sure that Joanne didn't quite know what to make of her and was therefore exercising caution. Jayne longed to better understand these soft-spoken people who lived on the reservation. She saw many subtle put-downs in town—so often that it almost seemed as if the "cowboys" really were at odds with the "Indians." It simply made no sense to have such strong divisions. She felt as if she had traveled back in time, and she couldn't understand why this town seemed so entrenched in such backward thinking. She even picked up on it occasionally in the classroom, but of course, it was much more subtle and innocent there. She tried to rein-force that they were all the same, created equally by the same loving God. The children responded well to this, and she only wished the adult community were as open-minded.

She drove out to the ranch early on Saturday morning, planning to finish up before noon and after that take some more quilted items over to the crafter's mall. Some of the ranchers were beginning to burn their wheat stubble, and the skies had taken on an almost eerie look. They were ghostly white and felt so low she thought she could reach up and touch them. The smell of smoke hung heavily in the air. She wondered if Harris had burned his stubble fields yet. She looked back to the recently harvested acreage but saw no plumes of smoke rising from the ground.

Nor did she see any signs of Harris, but that didn't surprise her. Maybe he was trying to send her a message. She was beginning to wonder if getting involved with Harris might be a case of too much too soon. And she didn't want to risk their exchange of Bailey's board as payment for helping with the livestock. Just to show him that there were no ill feelings on her part, she had made a batch of brownies last night, complete with walnuts. She planned to leave them with Jack, and hopefully Harris would see that she wasn't bothered by his aloofness.

"Hey, there!" she called from the back porch. "Anybody home?"

"Come in, Janie girl," said Jack as he slowly made his way toward the back door. "It's good to see you. I haven't talked to you all week."

"I've been meaning to stop and say hello, but each day seems to be shorter than the next, and before I know it it's nearly sunset, and I have to hurry to get Bailey put away before it's too dark."

"I see you've brought us some more goodies." Jack was eyeing the loaded paper plate.

"Sure did." She saw the coffeepot was half-full. "How about some coffee to go with them?"

Jack grinned. "I was hoping you'd ask."

She set the brownies on the table. "Go ahead and dive in,

Jack. I'll get our coffee." She saw that Jack was moving slower than usual today.

"I noticed a lot of farmers are burning their stubble fields today," said Jayne as she set a mug of coffee in front of Jack.

"Yep, it's that time of year."

"Do the fires ever get out of control?" Jayne was thinking of Bailey now. She didn't like the idea of his being out here without her to protect him if a wildfire arose. She didn't feel confident that Harris would worry too much about her half-breed horse.

"Nah, not too often. The main trick is to pay attention to the wind direction and keep plenty of water trucks on hand. It's pretty safe."

"I hope so. I worry about Bailey. I see those big plumes of smoke when I'm driving from town and imagine that the whole ranch is burning down." She felt Cowboy's nose sniffing her knee and then nudging her arm. She broke off a little piece of brownie and slipped it to him.

"Don't let it worry you, Janie. These ranchers know what they're doing. Now, these are some mighty tasty treats. You even put in nuts." Jack smacked his lips.

Jayne gave him a direct look. "So, Jack, how are *you* doing?"

"All right, I guess, for an old coot." Jack took another bite, then sighed. "Jayne, I haven't talked to you since you and Harris went out for dinner last week. I was so pleased that he was taking you, but I never heard nothing about how it all went. Harris was so tight-lipped about the whole thing...."

"We had a nice time, Jack."

"And?"

Jayne laughed. Despite his tough cowboy exterior, Jack did seem like an old woman sometimes. "And dinner was delicious."

"Come on, Janie, you've gotta give me more than that." Jack's brows were lifted in a gesture of appeal.

"I don't know what you want me to say."

"What do you think of my boy?"

Jayne laughed again. She could feel her cheeks beginning to glow. "I think Harris is a good man. He's a gentleman. And..." She couldn't think of anything else to say.

"And? Do you like him?"

"I feel like I'm in junior high. What do you mean, Jack? Of course I like him. Harris is a nice guy—"

Jack waved his hands back and forth and shook his head. "Oh, you young people! You think you have all the time in the world. Youth is wasted on the young. Okay, Janie girl, let me ask you this: are you going to go to dinner with Harris again?"

Jayne sighed and shrugged. "Sure, if he asks. But I don't think he will. I don't think he's ready for anything like...like you seem to be suggesting. He's hardly said more than a sentence to me all week."

"That's what I was afraid of, Janie. See, I think he's worried about getting involved and losing somebody. This is how he protects himself. I'm telling you, Janie, if you have any feelings for Harris, you're going to have to go after him and convince him that you aren't going to run away or kick the bucket—"

Jayne laughed. "How can anyone guarantee that they aren't going to 'kick the bucket'?"

Jack frowned. "I don't suppose they can. But you know what I mean."

"I'm not sure that I do, Jack." She finished her coffee. "But I tell you what—I'll give it some thought." She stood up and looked at him. "I know you're looking out for Harris's best interests, but Harris is a grown man. If he isn't interested in getting involved with anyone, you really shouldn't push him."

"I don't want to push him." Jack held up his hands then he grinned slyly. "I was just hoping you might give him a little nudge."

Jayne pretended to punch Jack in the arm, careful not to really hurt the old man. "Thanks a lot, Jack. At least you're laying your cards on the table."

Jack chuckled. "Well now, I might still have a card or two up my sleeve. You never know."

"Thanks for the coffee, Jack. It was fun chatting with you."

"Thanks for the brownies." Jack's eyes lit up. "Say, Harris is real fond of brownies. Maybe this will be just the little nudge I was looking for."

"Oh, Jack!" Jayne pretended to be exasperated, but she smiled as she headed toward the door. Cowboy was right on her heels, looking for more handouts. "I think Cowboy likes my brownies, too."

"That dog will eat anything!"

The next morning, Jayne went to Katherine's church. It was the second time she had come, and already she felt as though she belonged. The church met in a storefront on the run-down end of Main Street. The plate-glass windows were brightly painted, not very artistically, but at least they gave the worshipers more privacy. A team of three musicians played guitar, bass, and keyboard as they led a worship time that was both refreshing and inspiring.

Jayne glanced around the congregation as they sat attentively in folding metal chairs. They were an interesting mix of old and young, rich and poor, Native American and Caucasian. She wasn't even sure what denomination they were, or if it even mattered. The most important thing was that she was starting to feel at home with them. Pastor Conroy was an elderly man, but when he spoke he seemed much younger, and he seemed to understand the younger generation in a way that bridged the years. It wasn't that Jayne didn't love her own dad, but this was just the sort of man she would have loved to have had as a father. In some ways he reminded her of Jack, but with a deeper spirituality. She wasn't sure what Jack's views on religion were. She had not heard him speak of church, and his cowboy exterior made him seem a little hardened, but each time she spoke to him that tough shell seemed to disappear. What might Jack think of Pastor Conroy?

Today Pastor Conroy was talking about unity within the community and how it could only be accomplished through God's hands, but that God's hands often were the people who loved him. He spoke of healing and forgiveness and restoration, and while it sounded good and right, Jayne considered what it would really take to bring that kind of unity. Was it even possible?

"Something odd happened to me last night," said the pastor as he was bringing his sermon to a close. "While I was praying, I had what I would describe as a vision. I've never actually experienced this before, but I believe it was of God. I saw two young women who were teaching children on the reservation to love and serve God. I don't know what this means, but I know that I needed to share it. I think it was meant for someone in the congregation. But even as you hear me say this, you must ask yourself to listen, not to me, but to God. Only he can make clear what his will is for your life. I would deeply regret it if someone took my vision upon themselves and it wasn't really of God. To do this type of work would require commitment and time. It would be a ministry of love."

As the pastor finished speaking and then prayed for the

congregation, Jayne's chest grew tight and her heart began to beat wildly. She couldn't figure out what was wrong. Was God asking her to teach children on the reservation? She already taught kindergarten every day, and there were several reservation children in her class. Wasn't that enough? She silently debated back and forth for a few minutes, then finally she laid these thoughts before the Lord and asked him to lead and guide her.

After the service, Jayne treated Katherine and Autumn to an inexpensive lunch at the Burger Joint. They talked about school and horses and the crafter's mall, but Jayne did not mention that she was still pondering Pastor Conroy's vision. Afterward, Jayne went off to work with Bailey while the others stayed in town to do some errands. As Jayne drove through the reservation, she thought again about the children who lived there. She prayed that God would send someone to teach them. She imagined some older women, perhaps from the tribe. But still she felt a tugging at her heart. She enjoyed children, and it could be fun, but between her job and her horse, she was pretty busy. That wasn't even considering the time she was putting into caring for Harris's livestock or her quilting projects for the crafter's mall. Was it possible to do more?

She checked on the other animals, then worked with Bailey. He was getting so good at the commands and lead changes she had taught him in the last few weeks. She felt totally at ease on him and knew that he trusted her. "You are such a good, smart boy, Bailey," she said as she curried his coat in the area that was matted down from the saddle. She tried to always make certain that he was properly cooled off and brushed down after each ride, and he seemed to like the extra attention. She felt sure that he had never gotten it before. She was meticulous about checking his hooves and shoes. She had already had his hooves trimmed and was even considering a new set of shoes, since they were looking a little thin around the edges.

"Watch out, you're going to spoil him."

Jayne looked up to see Harris sitting on the top rail of the fence, with Cowboy seated on his haunches below as if they were both members of a little audience—or maybe a peanut gallery.

"I didn't hear you come up," she called as she threw her curry brush into her basket and turned to face him. She felt her cheeks grow warm as she walked over. "So, how have you been, Harris?"

"All right." He squinted off toward the setting sun. She followed his gaze with her eyes. The smoky skies had turned the sun into a bright shade of red, just the color of a ripe pomegranate. "How about you?"

"I'm doing great, thanks. I love this fall weather." She hoped to keep the conversation light and not reveal how she had felt ignored by him all week.

"That's good. Hopefully it'll hang around for a while. Have you had any trouble from the Long boy?"

She laughed. She could just imagine how irked Derrick would be to hear himself referred to as a boy. "No, I haven't. It's been quite a relief. I think he's given up."

"Well, that's good. For you, I mean."

She wasn't sure what to say next. She didn't want him to think she was just hanging around waiting for him to say or do something. It wasn't as if she didn't have things to do. She wasn't exactly sure what, but she knew she must have something. If nothing else, she could always go home and unpack her boxes. For some reason unpacking had turned into a giant mental block. She just couldn't make herself do it. She was afraid if she did, it would be admitting that she really lived in that horrible little apartment. And that was something she just couldn't do, not yet. She looked toward her car as though she were about to go, but then Harris began to speak, almost haltingly, as if he didn't really want to say the words that were coming out.

"A friend of mine, he's having a cattle drive next weekend. And, well, it looks like you've almost got that Arab of yours into shape. I was wondering if you'd like to tag along. It'll start in the mountains—on Friday night. Then we'll drive them down. I'm inviting Katherine and Autumn as well."

"Sure, that sounds like fun. But I'd have to get Bailey reshod first." She hoped her voice didn't reveal the excitement she felt. She wanted to keep things low-key. Partly for Harris, and partly for herself.

"Well, I've got the horseshoer out here the first part of the week, so I'll have him do Bailey too. And, uh, well, I know how you like to use all that English riding stuff, but I was wondering—if you'd like to borrow some western tack and a saddle…well, I've got some extras in the tack room."

She frowned at him for a moment, then reconsidered. It probably would be silly to use her English gear for a cattle drive. "Sure, that'd be fine. Do you suppose I could borrow a saddle this week to help Bailey make the adjustment?"

"Sure, that's a good idea." Harris seemed to answer too quickly, as if he were greatly relieved to think that she wouldn't be riding around in his pasture with her English gear. It all seemed so ridiculous, but apparently it was still a big deal to him.

"Do you want to show me which saddle I can use?"

"Sure, have you got time?"

"All the time in the world." As soon as she said it, she remembered her earlier resolve to appear cool and aloof. But when she saw his blue eyes twinkle, she didn't care. She never had liked playing games anyway.

ELEVEN

"Are you all ready for the big weekend?" asked Katherine.

"I think so," said Jayne as she sternly shook her head at Kenny Bunker to let him know she had seen him poking Lacy Green as they lined up to go inside from recess. "Bailey has adjusted pretty well to the western saddle, but it's not nearly as comfortable as the English. And I guess I've got the right kind of gear. Hopefully I won't humiliate Harris with my riding clothes—I'm going completely western."

Katherine laughed. "Look out for cowgirl Jayne!"

"That's right." Jayne hooked her thumbs in her belt and stuck her chin out for emphasis. "Oh, yeah, and Harris said that he'll trailer Bailey with his horse, Smoke, so I think that's all settled." She took a quick head count to make sure all the children were in line. "Okay, class, let's go inside now." She turned to Katherine. "I'll catch you after school. I want to check with you to make sure I've packed everything I need."

"All right," said Katherine. "Settle down, Jeremy," she warned, then winked at Jayne. "I'll see you later."

Finally the school day ended, and Jayne ushered her last pupil out the door. As usual it was Leah Bluefish. Jayne didn't mind because she was quite fond of Leah. She didn't want to have teacher's pets, but if the truth were told Leah would be her favorite. She was a quiet, serious little girl with big dark eyes. Jayne could tell that Leah longed for attention, but unlike some children who became very demanding to get it, Leah often hung back, watching with wide eyes. So Jayne always made a special effort to draw Leah out, encouraging her to speak up when she had an answer and choosing her to be the leader in certain activities. Jayne had met Leah's parents at open house. They were also very quiet. The mom, like Leah, was withdrawn and timid, but the dad, though quiet, had a dark, almost smoldering countenance, as if he had a large chip on his shoulder. Jayne was fairly certain that she'd smelled alcohol on him, and she knew this was not an uncommon problem with many men on the reservation. In fact, she was surprised, but grateful, that he had even come.

"Hey there," said Katherine. "Time to quit daydreaming and pack it up."

Jayne looked up from where she was sitting at her desk. "I guess I was zoning out a little."

"Anything serious?"

"Not with me. I was just thinking about Leah Bluefish."

"Sweet Leah. She is such a little doll."

"Do you know anything about her family?"

Katherine rolled her eyes. "Unfortunately, I probably know too much. It's not exactly what you'd consider a happy home. Her mom, Mary, went to school with me, and she was always a mousy sort of girl, but nice enough. And she wasn't stupid. But her dad was a mean old cuss. No one was very surprised when she married Lee Bluefish because he was so much like her dad. But it's still sad. I heard they were having some pretty bad problems, and that he may be seeing another woman. For Mary's sake, I hope he leaves her. She'd be better off without him."

Jayne nodded. "That's too bad for Leah, though. It would be hard on her to see her family break up."

"Yeah. But sometimes it comes down to the lesser of two

evils. There's a lot you don't understand about my people, Jayne."

"I know. But I'd like to." She shoved some papers into her bag and stood. "Have you eaten yet? Want to get some lunch?"

"Sure. I told Harris we'd be out there around two. We can pick up Autumn after we eat. She knows I'm getting her out of school early."

They drove into town to the little bakery and deli and ordered soup and bread. The smells of garlic and herbs made Jayne realize how hungry she was. They sat down at a gingham-covered table. It was a warm, cozy place for lunch, and the soup and bread were always delicious. As they waited for their order, Jayne quickly went over what she had packed for the cattle drive.

"Sounds like you did well, Jayne. Except that you might also need some sort of long rain slicker just in case the weather turns—that can happen quickly up in the mountains."

Jayne tried to think if she had a slicker that would work well on horseback. "Maybe I should go buy something."

"No, don't waste your money. I think I have an old one you can borrow.

The clerk at the counter called Jayne's name, and she went to get their order. She set it on the table before them and smiled at Katherine. She was thankful again that God had brought such a special friend into her life. What would she do without Katherine?

As they ate, the conversation turned to school and their students. "Jayne, I hope I didn't sound too negative about Leah's family. I guess I just get so tired of seeing reservation families with problems like that."

"Well, those problems aren't just limited to the reservation. It's a nationwide epidemic from what I hear."

"I know. But statistically, problems like alcohol are more prevalent on the reservation. Did you know that some researchers believe that it has to do with a chemical in the brain? And they say this chemical imbalance is more prevalent in Native Americans."

"I've never heard that. Do you think it's true?"

"I don't know. But sometimes I wonder."

Jayne took a sip of the fresh mushroom soup. "Katherine, do you remember what Pastor Conroy said last Sunday?"

Katherine looked at Jayne curiously. "You mean his sermon?"

"No. I mean what he called his vision."

Katherine nodded with a sober expression. "Yes. I remember. Why?"

"Well, I've been thinking and praying about it a lot. It's sort of haunting me. And then this thing about Leah and her family…well, I don't know, but I wonder if I'm supposed to be one of those women."

Katherine reached across the table and laid her hand on Jayne's arm. "Me too," she said, her dark eyes intense. "I can't quit thinking about it. I almost told you earlier this week, but I wanted to mull it over for a while. To make sure. Now that I know you're thinking along the same lines, I feel somewhat encouraged. But I have to admit, it still seems overwhelming."

"I know what you mean. But if we did it together, it might be fun. I've been thinking about some sort of 4-H-type Bible club or something. Maybe we could do crafts, or something to do with horses—"

"Right! And there's pottery, and I also do a little weaving and beadwork. You know, so many of our reservation kids really aren't learning the old crafts that the elders display at the root festivals and powwows. Perhaps there are ways to incorporate some of these traditional activities with the gospel."

"I'm sure there are."

"It would be something that Autumn would enjoy too. It might be a way for her to connect with the reservation kids."

"You mean she's not already friends with them?"

"Not very many. Some folks don't treat 'half-breeds' too kindly."

"I didn't know." Jayne felt her brows knit into a frown. "Actually, I didn't know that Autumn wasn't full Native American. I guess I never gave it much thought. Now that you mention it, her hair isn't as dark as yours. But I have seen other Native Americans with varying shades of hair."

Katherine nodded. "I think many of our people carry mixed blood. But the summer I got pregnant with Autumn, everyone knew it was with a certain white boy. I was young and stupid, and because of that, Autumn has to bear the stigma. And, of course, so do I. Not only that, but because I went away to college, I'm treated differently. Many people don't even speak to me. They think of me as an outsider now—like I'm white. Don't get me wrong, there are many good people in the tribe who don't think like that, but there are a fair number who can be cruel."

"Would it be any easier if you hadn't gone to college?"

"Goodness, no! It would've been much, much worse." Katherine smiled. "But you knew that, didn't you?"

"Well, I just couldn't imagine someone like you being happy living a life like Leah's mother must be living."

"You're right about that. In fact, if I were Mary and I wasn't a Christian, I'd probably do some serious damage to Lee Bluefish. But who knows, maybe if we start this Bible club thing with the kids we'll reach some parents as well."

"Wouldn't that be great?"

They finished lunch, then picked up Autumn. Katherine dropped Jayne off at Harris's to help load Bailey and Smoke. Jayne hadn't been around Smoke very much, but he seemed like a good horse. He was a large gray stallion with a strong head. After Jayne and Harris got the horses into the trailer, Harris lowered the tailgate for Cowboy. Jayne saw Cowboy's food and water dishes tucked alongside a bag of dog food and Harris's packed saddlebags. Cowboy easily leaped into the back of the pickup, his tail wagging. He looked at the two of them as if to say, "Okay, let's get going now." Harris closed the tailgate, and then went around and opened the passenger door for Jayne.

"Am I riding with you?" asked Jayne in surprise. She had thought she would be riding with Katherine and Autumn.

"Unless you want to walk. I told Katherine that we'd meet them up there. And we want to get there before dark so we can get the horses settled in."

Jayne climbed in and wondered what they would possibly talk about on the three-hour drive. She glanced at Harris as he slid behind the wheel, but he didn't seem concerned. "I meant to say thanks for the brownies you left at the house last week. Dad told me you made them." Harris looked at her, and his eyes twinkled as if he knew a secret joke.

"And what else did your dad tell you?" Jayne felt her cheeks beginning to burn. What had Jack said to him?

"Oh, you probably have a good idea. I swear, Dad is starting to act just like a little Cupid. I hope he hasn't been saying anything too wild to you. Don't pay too much attention to the old guy; he just needs to get out more, I think."

Jayne laughed. "I think you're right. He seems bound and determined to set you up with somebody, and desperate matchmakers can be the worst kind."

"Oh, I don't think he's desperate. He just thinks he knows what's best for me."

Jayne didn't know what to say to that and decided to change the subject. "So tell me about this friend of yours who needs his cattle driven."

"Paul Roderick." Harris sighed as if in serious thought. Jayne looked at his profile and admired again the firm jaw and the fine creases at the corners of his eyes. He had one of those faces that always looked interesting. It reminded her of the sky, always changing, but always nice to look at. Harris continued, "Well, Paul and I go way back. We went to grade school together. The first day I met this guy, I knew he was a cowboy. The way he walked and talked, even the way he smelled."

Jayne laughed. "You mean like a horse?"

"I suppose. Paul was a year older than me, and I practically worshipped him. He was the biggest, toughest kid around. I remember when he was in third grade, he fell from the top of the monkey bars and landed smack on his head—there was blood all over the place. Well, he stood right up and walked into the office. I heard he passed out when he got inside the building, but that was because he had a concussion. He never even cried."

Harris shook his head as if he was still impressed by this boyhood memory. "I thought Paul Roderick was tougher than nails. Then finally, during the summer when I was eleven and he was twelve we were in 4–H together and we became best buddies. His dad raised cattle; they used to own a bunch of land down here back then. But Paul's dad sold off some of it about ten years back and bought some timberland up in the hills for Paul to run cattle on. Paul said it was getting too popu-lated down here, and besides, the timber was a good invest-ment. Paul is a little on the hermit side. Anyway, that summer I spent every spare minute I could at their ranch. We roped and rode and even branded. We had us a heck of a time being cowboys. We stayed best friends right on through high school. We lost touch a little when I went to college. It was then that Paul talked his dad into investing in land up in the hills. Now I only see him once in a while. But it's always just like old times with us."

"He sounds like an interesting guy."

"He is. He never went to college, but he's one of the smartest men I know. He reads all the time. And he even writes cowboy poetry—but don't let him know that I told you. It's not something he talks about. Unfortunately, he's gone through some pretty tough times. He married his high-school sweetheart, a real nice gal named Sarah. They'd been married for about nine years when they found out she had cancer. He sent her everywhere for all kinds of treatment, but nothing worked. He nursed her during the last months of her life. She died two years ago."

"It sounds incredibly sad. Is he still grieving?"

"I'm hoping he's starting to pick up the pieces now. I go to see him whenever I can, and he's been in a pretty bad slump. He was letting his place go, but I think his family has stepped in to help some. It's the first time Paul's had a cattle drive since before Sarah got sick. This used to be a yearly event. So I take that as a good sign. I was real pleased to hear he was doing it again. Actually, it's a mutual friend of ours, Jim Scoggins, who's setting it all up. He's hoping it'll help to pull Paul out of this."

"Does Katherine know Paul?"

"Yep. Everyone in town knows Paul. He was our local cowboy hero. One of the best saddle-bronc riders ever to come out of this town. Sarah begged him to quit after he injured his back

one year, and of course, he would have done just about anything for that woman."

Harris grew quiet as he continued to drive. Jayne looked
out the window. They were getting into the wooded area of the
mountains now.

"It's beautiful up here," she said.

Harris nodded. "Yeah, I can understand why Paul wanted to
live up here. Too bad he has to live alone."

"What about his dad? Didn't you say he and his dad were
both into the cattle?"

"Financially, they're partners. But his parents still live in
town. His dad's got a lot of money, and they have a pretty full
social life. Paul's mother wouldn't have lasted a week up here
without all her clubs and things."

"I see. Sort of like Derrick's family."

"You got the picture. In fact, Paul's dad is pretty good
friends with Mr. Long."

"Well, Paul sounds like a really nice guy. I can't wait to meet
him."

"He is. I think you'll like him."

They drove in silence for a while. Jayne mulled over the fact
that Harris's best friend had also lost the woman he loved. That
must complicate things even more for Harris. Maybe Jack was
right, that Harris had a hard time getting seriously involved
with a woman because he'd lost his mother, his girlfriend, and
then witnessed Paul losing Sarah. How sad. Jayne looked over
at Harris and felt her heart give a little twinge. She knew that
she seriously liked him, but usually she was the one who was
pursued in a relationship. It had been a comfortable role, and
she wasn't ready for anything else. But Jack's words kept playing through her head.

Finally, she shot up a silent prayer, asking God to lead her in this relationship. She had no desire to get into something that wasn't God's will. She had already been burned by Derrick. And besides, she wasn't even sure that Harris was a Christian. Although she remembered that Derrick's claim to Christianity had given her a sense of security that had turned out to be false. Perhaps there were no strict rules in these things. And if that was the case, she needed God's direction now more than ever.

It was late afternoon and already getting cool as they slowly wound up the road. Jayne looked at the tall evergreens growing out of rugged hills. She breathed deeply of the pine-scented air, then shivered slightly as the cool air blew through her partially opened window.

"I hope you brought plenty of warm stuff," said Harris, interrupting her thoughts. "It can get pretty chilly up in the mountains at night."

"I was just thinking about that. And I did. Plus Katherine is bringing me a slicker in case it rains." Tall timber on each side cast long shadows across the road. Shadows and light, shadows and light. Just like ripples in a stream. She watched the rhythmic display, almost hypnotized by the repetition.

"I hope Bailey handles okay," she said a few minutes later. "This will be a new experience for him."

"How's the old boy taking to western?"

"Okay, I guess."

"He's probably relieved." Harris chuckled. "He probably felt like a sissy in that flimsy little saddle."

Jayne frowned. "I'm not so sure about that. Think about it, Harris. If you were a horse, which would you prefer? A heavy, stiff, clunky western saddle, or a lightweight, sleek English saddle?"

Harris didn't say anything. But that was answer enough. Jayne grinned. Harris turned off the main road to a narrow gravel road that seemed to go almost straight up.

"This is Paul's road, but it's still several miles to the house."

"Wow, it's a good thing you have such a strong pickup. Do you think Katherine will have any trouble with her old clunker?"

Harris smiled. "That old clunker might look like a bunch of junk, but it's got one tough engine under the hood."

"How do you know?"

"It used to be mine. I sold it to Katherine when she moved back out here. I had just rebuilt the engine. And believe me, it can climb this hill with no problem."

Finally they pulled into a flat area with a ranch house, barn, corrals, and several other outbuildings. They were surrounded by a large hay meadow, and everything was nestled in the midst of hilly timberland and mountains. The buildings were all bat-and-board siding with red metal roofing. The family brand was handsomely displayed over the big barn. It reminded Jayne of something from an old western movie.

"This is incredibly lovely!" she said as Harris pulled the trailer in next to the corral.

He grinned. "You might not want to say that to Paul."

"I guess *lovely* isn't exactly the right word. But it is charming and old-fashioned. What a wonderful place to live."

They got out, then unloaded the horses and led them to the corral.

"Hey, Bailey, how was the ride back there?" said Jayne as she stroked his nose. Bailey sniffed the air of his new surroundings, then snorted loudly. "Are you ready for this, boy? I hope the other horses are nice to you."

Harris laughed. "You act like he's human."

Jayne looked at Harris in surprise. "Well, maybe he is to

me. And there's nothing wrong with talking to your horse. Maybe you should try it sometime."

Harris shook his head. She felt a little foolish but told herself that she was perfectly normal. Bailey liked hearing her voice and responded well to her words.

"You want out of there, Cowboy?" asked Harris as he let down the tailgate.

"What?" said Jayne. "Are you actually talking to your dog?"

Harris's brow creased, and suddenly she wished she hadn't teased him. Then he grinned. "I guess I see your point."

They walked the horses over to the lodgepole corral. Jayne spotted fresh hay and a full water trough. "Looks like they're expecting company," she said more to Bailey than to Harris. Smoke and Bailey both ambled over to the hay and began munching contentedly.

"Hey, Harris!"

Harris turned. "Paul!" He walked over to the man standing on the other side of the yard, and they clasped hands for a long moment, slapping each other on the shoulders. Then Harris turned and nodded to Jayne. "Paul, I want you to meet Jayne."

She walked quickly over and shook hands with Paul. He was a big man with a strong handshake. His eyes and hair were strikingly dark, and his face had the look of someone who had been through some hard times. "It's a pleasure to meet you, Paul. And thank you for allowing me to come on this cattle drive. I hope you don't mind greenhorns—both me and my horse."

Paul smiled, and his teeth flashed white. "No problem. We usually have one or two greenhorns on every drive. Everybody has to start somewhere. But we don't put up with any whining or complaining." Paul eyed her carefully as if measuring her up.

"Oh, I don't think you need to worry about Jayne," said

Harris. "Her looks might fool you, but she's pretty tough underneath."

Jayne glanced quickly at Harris. "Thanks, I think." The two men laughed.

"You guys are the first ones here," said Paul. "Besides Jim, that is. Jim's in the barn getting some things together."

"Should we go give him a hand?" asked Harris.

"Probably. Jayne, you can go on in the house, if you like. Jim's bride, Amy, is in there working on some kind of food thing." He turned to Harris. "My baby brother, Adam, is coming with a few friends. A few of the old-timers couldn't make it this trip, so I guess it's time for some new blood."

Harris chuckled. "I remember the first time Adam made this trip—first and last as I recall. I didn't think he'd ever want to try it again."

"Well, I guess his friends talked him into it. Hopefully it'll go better for him this time around. And didn't you say you were bringing a couple others?"

"Katherine Patawa and her daughter. They should be here soon."

"Wow, I can't believe Katherine's daughter is old enough to go on a cattle drive." Paul rubbed his chin. "The last time I saw that little girl, she was toddling around in diapers."

"Well, Autumn is a pretty good horsewoman now. I think she'll be just fine on the drive." Harris turned to Jayne. "I guess we'll catch up with you later, Jayne."

"Make yourself at home, Jayne," said Paul as the two men headed off toward the barn. Jayne felt a little like the odd man out, or maybe it was odd woman, but she decided to go and meet Amy, reminding herself that this was the West, and perhaps men still thought women were relegated to the kitchen. Well, she could play that role, at least for a couple of days.

"Hello," she called as she entered the front door. No one answered, and she poked her head into the living area. The house was woodsy looking, with open-beamed timbers and natural pine floors. She could see that it was a nice home, but without a woman's touch it looked somewhat cluttered and neglected. But the general layout and the style of furnishings were pleasant, with a couple of leather couches comfortably arranged in front of a large rock fireplace, and one wall full of windows, looking out on the meadow behind the corral. Not far off in the background were the mountains.

"Hi," said a female voice. "Isn't that view amazing?"

Jayne turned. "You must be Amy. And yes, it's incredible. No wonder Paul chose to live up here." Jayne studied the petite blond woman and wondered if she were going on the cattle drive too. She didn't look sturdy enough to make what Jayne expected to be a rigorous two-day ride. "I'm Jayne. I came with Harris."

Amy's eyes twinkled. "Ahh. It's about time Harris started getting involved with a woman."

"Oh, it's not like that." Jayne felt her cheeks redden. "I keep my horse at Harris's place, and I help with the animals—"

"I'm sorry, I didn't mean to sound like Yentl. It's just that we all worry about Harris. It's fine to be friends." Amy's eyes twinkled again. "Some of the best relationships start out that way. Anyway, I'm glad you're here, Jayne. It's nice to have some other females along. Maybe it'll help distract us from the fact that this is the first cattle drive since Sarah passed away. Harris probably told you that it was an annual tradition with a bunch of us—but for the last several years, since Sarah got sick, Paul has hired an outfit to bring them down. Maybe this will be the beginning of a new era for Paul. It's time for him to move on with his life."

"Well, I hope this helps. Katherine and Autumn are coming, too. I suppose you know them?"

"Yes. Katherine's been a regular on these drives, although she's never brought her daughter along. I hope it's not too much for the girl. But Katherine is a smart lady, she wouldn't bring her daughter up if she didn't think she could handle it. Katherine had our youngest son in her class last year. She's such a wonderful person. Well, Jim says I could talk the hind leg off of a mule, and I guess I probably should get back to my KP duty if we're going to have any dinner tonight."

"Let me give you a hand," said Jayne as they moved into the next room. "This looks like a great kitchen."

"Yes, Sarah planned it well. It's got everything you could ever want. Sarah knew that being out in the boonies like this, she would need to be pretty self-sufficient. And she always was prepared for crowds. She got an ironstone set of twenty-four place settings just for times like this."

"She sounds like a nice person."

Amy swallowed. "She was."

Jayne and Amy worked together quietly for a while, but before long Amy was chattering away again, hardly stopping to breathe. She proved a good source of information about some of the old cattle drive regulars. Soon Katherine and Autumn arrived and pitched in as well. They could hear other people arriving, followed by the sound of doors opening and closing, and voices and laughter. It sounded as if an exciting weekend lay ahead, and Jayne was thankful for this wonderful new group of friends.

They planned to eat a big dinner and then turn in early, spending the first night at the ranch. Then everyone would get up very early, before daybreak, and ride up to where the cattle were. The actual drive would start then, as they gathered and pushed the cattle down the mountain and out of the timber to the wild grass acreage below. Jayne could hardly wait.

The food was finally ready, and Jayne was carrying a large bowl of mashed potatoes out to the long wooden table when she heard a familiar voice speaking loudly.

"Howdy there, Jim boy. Say, thanks for letting us horn in on this little get-together. I've never done anything like this, but it sounds like a real hoot."

Jayne froze in her tracks, then forced herself to quietly place the bowl on the table. She glanced toward the front door, and sure enough, there was Derrick, shaking hands with Jim and going on about the drive and how great it would be. She felt her heart pounding hard. Oh, why did he have to be here? Just when she was looking forward to a really fantastic weekend. She felt as though someone had just punched her in the stomach. She quickly turned and slipped back into the kitchen without being seen.

"What's wrong?" asked Katherine when she saw Jayne's face. "You look ill."

"I am," said Jayne. She slumped into a kitchen chair. "Derrick is here," she said quietly, not wanting Amy to overhear.

Katherine's face fell, and she sank into a chair across from Jayne. "You're kidding!"

"I wish I were. What am I going to do?"

Katherine thought for a long moment, her dark eyes narrowed and her lips pressed tightly together. Finally she said in a firm voice, "Jayne, you are going to buck up and act like nothing whatsoever is wrong. You are going to sit tall in the saddle, keep a stiff upper lip, and shoot from the hip."

They both began to giggle. Then Katherine grew serious again. "Remember, you are Harris's guest on this drive. And

Harris is Paul's best friend. You have every right in the world to be here, and if anyone should feel awkward, it should be Derrick."

Jayne smiled weakly at Katherine, feeling encouraged. "You're absolutely right, Katherine. Thanks, I needed that."

TWELVE

◆

After dinner was finally over, Jayne went to check on Bailey and Smoke. They seemed fine. She had also sneaked out a bone for Cowboy, which he happily carried back under the pickup where he was sleeping. Jayne went back inside and found Katherine and Autumn in the room the three of them would share for the night.

While Autumn was in the bathroom, Jayne thanked Katherine again for her predinner pep talk. "I can't believe how easily it went. I just took your advice, and thankfully I didn't have to shoot from the hip."

Katherine laughed. "You did great. And I don't know if you had a chance to see Derrick's face, but you definitely came out on top. He looked as if he had seen a ghost. And Corky, well, I had to keep myself from laughing. She looked fit to be tied. Her face matched her red hair."

Jayne laughed. "Well, I feel sorry for Corky, but she'll have to find out sooner or later what he's really like. I just hope that everything goes well on the drive. It shouldn't be too difficult to keep distance between us; after all, that's a pretty big mountain."

"Yes, and I heard Harris say that he'll be riding with us. So we shouldn't need to worry about Derrick Long."

"That will help me sleep better. And thanks for all the moral support, Katherine. I don't know what I'd do without you."

"That's what friends are for."

"Well, I hope I'm as good a friend to you. You never seem to have any major problems."

Katherine laughed. "You just haven't known me long enough." Then she grew serious. "Hey, I told Autumn about the kid's ministry thing. She was so excited, I could hardly believe it. Now I feel as if I have to do it. I hope you haven't changed your mind, Jayne."

"Not at all. In fact, the more I think about all the things we can do to draw them in, like your pottery and weaving, and my quilts and crafts—"

"Are you guys talking about Bible Club?" asked Autumn as she came into the bedroom.

"That's right, honey," said Katherine. "Do you think it should be called Bible Club?"

"Uh-huh," said Autumn as she climbed into her sleeping bag on the floor. "But we can tell the kids that there will be a lot of other things, too."

"What do you think, Jayne?"

"I cast my vote with Autumn."

"Well, it's unanimous then," said Katherine as she clicked out the light. "Good night, girls. Get plenty of rest. Believe me, you'll need it."

The alarm seemed to go off just moments after they had gone to sleep, but Jayne was eager for the day to begin. She was also concerned about how Bailey had fared being around strange horses. She dressed quickly and hurried outside to check on him. It was dark, but she went over to the corral and clicked her tongue the way she always did to get his attention. He came ambling over and nudged her gently with his nose.

"Hi there, sweet thing," she said as she rubbed his neck. She put her face close to him and breathed in deeply, enjoying the earthy, warm smell of horsehide and dust. "Looks like you made it through the night. Did any of those old quarter horses give you a bad time?"

"Here she is, talking to her horse again." Jayne turned and made out the form of Harris in the dim light. "Jayne, don't you know that he doesn't understand a word you say?"

"I don't know any such thing. In fact, I'm pretty certain that if he doesn't understand the exact words, he certainly understands the meaning behind them."

Harris laughed quietly. "You beat all."

"Well, think about it. How much of communication are the actual words? And how much are the tone and mannerisms?"

Harris didn't answer.

"For instance, I could say to you…" She paused to think of the right words, then said in a sarcastic tone, "Gee, you sure look great today, Harris. You must've slept real well."

He frowned at her.

"Now listen—" She drew closer and this time spoke in a sweet voice. "Gee, you sure look great today, Harris. You must've slept real well."

He said nothing for a long moment. She felt his eyes on her, almost as if he had forgotten this was only an experiment, an example to make her point. He cleared his throat and stepped back. "I guess I see what you mean. I suppose you might have something there, Jayne." He looked over his shoulder to see if anyone had been watching, then said in a casual tone, "So, are you all ready for the big day?"

"I guess so. I hope I don't drag anyone down."

The first light of day was creeping into the meadow, and a few early birds were beginning to sing. The other horses saw them standing there and came over, nickering for their breakfasts. Harris and Jayne tossed some hay over the fence, and then stood and watched for a while as the animals began to munch hungrily.

"Well, we'd better go get some breakfast," said Harris. "I

heard that Joyce Rivers and Corky Galloway are on KP this morning. I know Joyce can cook, but I have my doubts about Corky."

"Maybe I should go help out."

"Nah," said Harris. "They'll be fine."

"Who cooks on the ride?"

"Everyone helps out."

"Even the guys?"

Harris nodded. "Yep, and sometimes I think the guys are the best cooks out there."

"Well, it's nice to think there might be some liberated men in the West."

"Just don't let 'em hear you talking like that, Jayne."

She couldn't tell if he was joking or not, but she decided not to ask. Fortunately, breakfast was edible. Corky made plenty of noise about not knowing how to cook and not wanting to learn. Everyone teased her as they dug through her lopsided stack of odd-shaped pancakes, searching for ones that were neither black nor runny.

Finally, they were all packed up and on horseback. They broke into five small groups, each with five or six members, and each with a designated trail boss. Paul and Jim each led a group, and a man named Allen led another. As expected, Harris was the trail boss for Jayne, Katherine, and Autumn; and a teenaged boy named Jason, who was Jim and Amy's nephew, joined them. Jayne was surprised to hear that Derrick would be leading a group. She had always thought her riding was better than his. Of course, now she was riding western and on rugged terrain, so she couldn't allow herself to become overconfident.

All the groups departed, heading to where the herd had spent the spring and summer. Even though it was only mid-

October, there was a heavy frost on the ground, and Jayne was glad she had brought plenty of warm clothes. Overhead, the sky was perfectly clear and a brilliant shade of robin's egg blue. The smell of pine was invigorating. Jayne thought this must be one of the most beautiful places on earth.

After crossing several rushing streams, it looked as if Autumn would have no problem keeping up with Red beneath her. Both Bailey and Red were complete gentlemen when it came to crossing water. Jayne glanced over at Jason. He was gawky on a horse, but at least he had a sense of humor, and when he almost got wiped out by a low branch, he just laughed and made light of his failure to duck in time. Cowboy looked as though he was having a great time, with no problem keeping up. He didn't seem to mind that his normally shiny coat was now full of dust and weeds. With his pink tongue lolling out the side of his mouth, he looked as though he was smiling. All in all, it was a very pleasant morning. Just before noon, they reached their destination point, the lower herd of cattle.

Harris got on his walkie-talkie and advised Paul of their whereabouts. "We'll let the horses have a good drink here," he told the group as he pointed to a nearby stream. "Then we're all meeting up on Hampton Ridge for lunch. It's just a short hike up that rock rim." He pointed to a small hill. "But it'll be quicker to leave the horses here, plus they'll have a chance to cool off. Jim's group is in charge of lunch today. We may have to do some rearranging of the groups up there. Seems that Derrick's group is having some trouble. Apparently there was some disagreement on directions, and the group broke up. Half the group are already on the ridge with Jim, but Derrick and Corky are still coming."

Jayne tried not to laugh. She hoped Derrick didn't mess

things up for the rest of them. She securely tied Bailey to a pine tree, allowing him plenty of rope so he could graze on the abundant bunchgrass around him. "Now don't overdo it. You still have a long ride this afternoon," she said as she removed the saddle and set it nearby.

"What are you doing?" asked Harris as he came over.

She looked up. "What do you mean?"

"Why are you taking his saddle off now?"

"So he can cool off. You said the horses are going to be here awhile."

"It won't hurt your horse to keep his saddle on."

"That's your opinion. I don't mind taking extra care with him. He's not used to wearing a saddle all day. And especially this heavy western one—"

"You'll be thankful for that saddle once the real riding begins." Harris turned, then tossed over his shoulder, "You can't always baby him, Jayne." He walked toward where the others were already starting to head up the ridge.

Jayne sighed. Would she ever learn to keep her thoughts to herself? Why did she always go into battle when it came to her horse? Sure, to Harris he was just a horse. But to her, Bailey was a friend. Why couldn't Harris understand that? She told herself to let it go. She pulled her water bottle out of the saddle-bag and took a long, cool drink. She noticed Cowboy panting at her feet and offered him some water too.

Just as she hadn't allowed Derrick to get to her last night, she wouldn't allow Harris to get to her now. What was it with guys, anyway? Why couldn't men be more like horses?

She followed the group from a distance, thankful for some time to herself. But as the others began climbing up the rocks, Harris turned back to join her. *Great,* she thought, *here comes another lecture on horses.*

"I thought you might want some company," Harris called in a friendly voice.

She looked down at Cowboy. She thought the dog was pretty good company. Then she shrugged and walked toward Harris.

"Jayne, I didn't mean to rub you the wrong way with your horse. I guess you need to do what you think is best. After all, he's your horse. I'll try to stay out of it."

"Thanks. I probably do baby him, but he's such an important part of my life. I mean, you have lots of horses and other animals, and your farm. Bailey sometimes seems like the only thing I have." Suddenly she wished she hadn't said that. It sounded so pitiful. "That is, I have teaching and friends, but Bailey came to me just when I needed him. He was like a gift from God."

"Jayne, you don't have to explain everything to me. But I guess I understand. I just don't know if it's good to let your heart get so attached to any one thing. I mean, he's just a horse. He could fall and break a leg—"

"Don't say that!"

"Well, it could happen. This is a rough ride. But I'm sure he'll be fine. I'm just saying that when you love something that much, you could get hurt."

She turned to study Harris. Even in the shadow of his cowboy hat, she could see his creased brow, his eyes looking intently ahead. His chin jutted out to add emphasis to his words. They sounded as if they had been spoken from his heart, although she suspected he wasn't really talking about horses.

"So are you saying that it's better to love something *less* just in case that something is taken from you—and that will make it hurt less?"

He stopped in his tracks and looked at her curiously. "I don't claim to know a lot about these things, Jayne. I'm just saying that animals come and go. You shouldn't treat them like people."

"What about people?"

"Huh?"

"Don't they come and go, too?"

Harris turned back toward the trail and continued walking, taking long strides. "I suppose so," he muttered just loud enough for her to hear.

Jayne hurried to keep up. She couldn't think of anything to say. Already she felt as if she were needling him. Finally they reached the rim and began to hike up. She had paused at a spot that was fairly steep, trying to decide which rocks to step on, when Harris reached out and stuck out a hand.

She smiled up at him. "Thanks. Now I can see why we didn't bring the horses."

He gripped her hand firmly in his and easily pulled her up to the top of a large boulder. "The others came around the south side on horseback. But they're heading up to the higher pasture anyway. Since we're bringing down the lower cows, there was no sense in bringing the horses all the way up here and then back down again."

"So you do think about what's good for the horses. Are you sure that's not babying them?"

"Using good sense to watch out for your critters is a lot different than singing them to sleep and kissing them good night."

Jayne laughed. Had he seen her kiss Bailey? Well, she didn't care. She had nothing to hide, and she wasn't ashamed that she loved her horse.

"Hey, you slowpokes!" called Katherine. "We thought maybe you were pulling a Derrick and Corky on us. Lost in the wilderness!"

Jayne threw her a look that said she didn't think that was

funny. "Is lunch ready? I'm starving."

"You should see it," said Autumn. "Barbecued beef, corn on the cob, potato salad—everything!" Autumn looked charming with her hair messy and her hat hanging down her back by a stampede string. Her golden red skin, lighter than her mother's, contrasted nicely against her turquoise shirt.

"How did they get that all up here?" asked Jayne.

"Yesterday Jim and Paul brought pack mules to each of the camp spots, loaded with a lot of stuff," said Harris. "Then they got the fire pits all set up so it's pretty easy to get food cooking."

"Sounds like they have this down to a science," said Jayne.

"Yep, and by the smell of that food, I'd say it's also a bit of an art." Harris grinned at her.

The other riders began trickling in. Some looked a little weary, but once they saw the food cooking, they began to perk up. Jim's group was in charge of lunch, and Jayne was pleased to see that petite Amy was holding up just fine. She was tossing orders at the group members, and from the way they were hurrying to follow them, Jayne guessed that it would only be a matter of minutes before lunch was served.

"Everything is ready now, but should we wait for Derrick and Corky?" asked Amy.

Jim looked at Paul, and Paul thought for a moment, then looked around at the hungry group. "No, it won't do them any good if the rest of us are starving." He looked back at Jim. "I know we haven't ever done this before, but you know since I lost Sarah, I've been living a little differently. Jim, I wondered if you could ask a blessing for this meal."

Jim grinned. "You bet I can." He bowed his head. Jayne noticed surprised looks on some of the faces, but everyone lowered their heads. "Dear mighty God," he began in a loud voice. "Thank you for this glorious creation, the sky, the trees, the mountains. And we thank you for these dear friends, especially our brother Paul. We ask for your blessing and protection. We thank you for this fine meal, Lord, and ask that you bless it. We also ask that you help Derrick and Corky to find their way. Amen."

Many amens were heard, and before long everyone had a loaded plate and a place to sit and eat. Jayne was already half finished by the time Paul came over and sat down next to Harris. Paul turned to Jayne and Katherine.

"How are you ladies holding up?" he asked as he took a bite of potato salad.

"I'm doing fine," said Katherine. "And Autumn is holding her own."

Paul smiled at Autumn. "I noticed that. You're quite a good horsewoman. You seem very comfortable in the saddle."

Autumn smiled shyly. "I've been riding ever since I can remember."

"That's the best way to do it. That's the way my pop taught me."

Katherine looked at Autumn, then back to Paul. "And you can take it from him, Autumn. He's one of the best. I used to watch him ride some of the wildest broncs at the rodeo."

"You rode at Roundup?" Autumn's eyes grew wide.

Paul nodded. "That was a long time ago. Another lifetime."

"Wow, that's cool," said Autumn. "I want to be a barrel racer. I've been practicing a lot."

"That's great. You keep it up, Autumn. Maybe we'll be seeing you riding in a rodeo someday." He took another bite of barbecue.

"I hope so." Autumn was grinning widely, and Jayne realized that was something Autumn rarely did, even before she had gotten braces on her teeth. But today those silver wires were gleaming in the sunshine.

"So, Paul," said Harris, "Jim said you were going to reorganize the groups. What do you have in mind?"

Paul pushed his cowboy hat back on his head and looked around the group. "Well, I was thinking maybe Jason here should be riding with his Uncle Jim. And the Petersons wanted to join Allen's group anyway."

"That leaves Derrick and Corky, your baby brother, Adam, and his girlfriend, Tracy. What do you plan to do with them?"

Paul shook his head. "This is where you come in. You see, Adam still wants to be in Derrick's group because Tracy and Corky are such good friends. But I don't think it would be wise to have my brother in my group. So…"

"You want me to do some baby-sitting?"

"Oh, I wouldn't call it that. Corky is good on a horse. And Derrick, well, he's okay. From what Adam says, Tracy can hold her own."

"But that makes for a pretty large group here." Harris looked at Jayne. She suspected that he knew she wasn't too thrilled about this new arrangement.

Paul tossed his bare corncob into the trees. "Well, I can take Katherine and Autumn with my group—"

"Great!" said Autumn.

Jayne threw Katherine a look, hoping that she would help out, but Katherine wasn't looking her way. Katherine's eyes were fixed on Paul. Jayne didn't know what to do. She looked desperately at Harris, but he just shrugged his shoulders and lifted his brows.

"Okay, but what do I do if Derrick pulls another stunt like this?"

"I don't think he will," said Paul. "If he does, just send him home."

Harris chuckled. "Now wouldn't that be something. Well, here they come now." Harris took his plate and got up for seconds.

Jayne looked over to see Derrick and Corky ride up. Corky jumped off her horse and walked quickly over to the group. Jayne could tell by the way Corky walked that she was exasperated at Derrick. Corky spoke to Tracy, glancing over her shoulder at Derrick, who was just now getting off his horse. For a split second, Jayne almost felt sorry for Derrick.

"Well, if we're riding with you," Katherine said to Paul, "we'd better get our horses and bring them up here so we'll be ready."

"I'll go tell Derrick about the new plan," said Paul.

Harris returned with a full plate. Jayne wanted to go back for seconds too, but Derrick and Corky were getting their food now. She looked over at Harris. "Couldn't you have done something to prevent this?"

He put his hands in the air. "What?"

She shook her head, then looked down at her empty plate. "I don't know. Anything."

"Jayne, I was trying to think of an excuse, but nothing came to me. I'm just not as quick with answers as you are."

"What does that mean?"

"Oh, you know how you always have an answer for everything."

Jayne studied him. His eyes were as blue as the October sky and they were looking intently at her. "Do I come across like that? Like a smart mouth, I mean?"

Harris laughed. "I don't think of you as a smart mouth. But you are a smart lady, and you have quick wits about you. Sometimes you remind me of my old man. He's got a pretty fast tongue."

She smiled at him. "Well, thank you. I'll take that as a compliment. But if I have to put up with anything from Derrick, I expect some intervention from the trail boss."

"It would be my pleasure."

The sun and the sky were brilliant and the vistas were crystal clear. It was the hottest part of the day, and Cowboy was making the most of the lunch break by taking a nap in the shade. Jayne wished she could join him.

"And now I'm going to gather my new group and tell them what the plan is," said Harris. "Coming?"

"I can hardly wait." Jayne followed Harris, and they made their way over to where Derrick and Corky were sitting.

Corky and Derrick were just starting to eat. Harris called Tracy and Adam over to join them. "Okay, guys, Paul has put you into my group. And while we want to have a good time—" he looked directly at Derrick—"we're here to do a job as well. Jayne will be riding with me. And I assume that Corky and Derrick will be—"

"Hold it, Harris," said Corky, holding one hand up. "Don't be so quick on the draw." She pointed to Tracy. "I'm riding with her."

Harris nodded. "That okay with you, Adam?"

Jayne looked at Adam. He didn't seem anything like Paul. He was shorter, more slightly built, and his hair was a faded brown. He shrugged. "I guess so."

Derrick said nothing, but Jayne saw the angry look in his eyes. She wanted to remind Derrick that he was a Christian. She had wanted to remind him of that at other times but knew it wasn't her place to judge.

"We'll meet you down at the lower meadow. You know how to find it?" Harris directed the question to Derrick.

"I know the way," said Adam.

"Good. We'll see you down there in an hour, okay?"

Derrick frowned. "We just got here—"

"Shut up, Derrick," said Corky.

Jayne couldn't help smiling when she and Harris walked away.

"I think maybe that boy has met his match in Corky," said Harris as soon as they were out of earshot.

"That is, if she doesn't dump him," said Jayne. "It's weird, but I almost feel sorry for him."

"You're kidding."

She shook her head. "It makes it easier to forgive him. And I'm finding that it's something I have to do again and again."

"Forgive him?"

"Yeah. It seems every time I see him, I have to do it. But each time is easier."

THIRTEEN

◆

I n the middle of the afternoon, Harris sent Jayne and Bailey out to gather some strays from a fairly steep ravine. Jayne thought it might have been his way of giving her space away from Derrick, and she didn't mind a bit. She found the cattle, about a dozen of them, nearly at the bottom. She paused for a moment on the rim, wondering if it would be too difficult to reach them. On the other side of the ravine were several deer: a few does along with their fawns. She decided if cattle and deer could climb down there, Bailey could too.

She nudged Bailey, and he began to maneuver down the rugged incline, carefully picking a trail before him. He seemed at ease, and Jayne tried to relax too. At one point he brushed a little too close to a scrubby juniper tree and her long braid became snagged by a branch. She stopped Bailey, and with some effort finally disengaged herself from the tree. When she was free, her neat braid was gone and her hair hung in a tangled mess down her back, with twigs and branches mixed in. Well, this was no time for vanity.

She looked down at the cattle again. They looked comfortably settled in a shady part of the ravine. Bailey continued, slowly moving toward the cattle as if he understood the nature of this mission. A couple of times she felt a hoof slip, but Bailey quickly recovered. At last they reached the cattle, but then the stubborn animals refused to move. She yelled and pushed Bailey against them, and slowly they started to walk up the ravine, bawling all the while. After what seemed like days, she finally drove the herd of stragglers into the larger herd. Harris waved at her from the other side, and they continued driving them down the mountain.

To everyone's relief, Harris's group managed to get their part of the herd down to the first station without any major problems. It turned out that Corky and Tracy made a strong pair, and they took directions well. Jayne was pleased with how Bailey handled, and she thought she and Harris made a pretty good team. They probably could have gotten by without the other two men in their group, but fortunately, Adam and Derrick didn't get into any real trouble.

When they finally got the herd settled into the new meadow, Harris told them it was their night to fix dinner. "And if we want to avoid a riot, we'd better get started right now."

"You've got to be joking!" Derrick looked at Harris with an expression one might use to complain to the waiter about the service.

Harris nodded to Adam. "Why don't you fill Derrick in." Before he walked away, he added, "And don't poke around, we need to get that fire going right away, boys."

Jayne heard Derrick grumble, but she was far enough away that she didn't catch the words. "What would you like me to do, boss?" she asked Harris cheerfully.

Harris smiled. "Now, that's what I like to hear. And by the way, you and Bailey did a good job out there today. I saw you push that stubborn pair out of the buck brush again and again."

Jayne smiled. "Thanks."

"And you didn't have any problem rounding up those strays out of the ravine?"

"Surprisingly, no. Bailey is more comfortable on the rugged terrain than I am. He did great."

"Bailey seems to be a lot stronger than I thought he was."

Jayne beamed. "And that's what I like to hear. Now tell me, what needs to be done around here?"

"Well, maybe you and the other ladies could start wrapping potatoes in foil. We'll bake them in the hot coals as soon as the boys get the fire going. There are supposed to be a bunch of game hens, all seasoned and wrapped in foil, in that big ice chest—they'll need to go on before the potatoes. Then there's fixings for a green salad. That's enough to keep you busy for now. You want to take the lead with the women?"

"Sure. Just don't make me have to give Derrick orders."

"Not a problem. I like doing that." Harris grinned.

Jayne had already had a couple of conversations with Corky and had discovered that she actually liked her. She wasn't a complainer, she was a hard worker, and she was good on a horse. Corky and Tracy were setting up camp. Jayne was relieved to see that the two of them were sharing a tent. She knew that neither of these couples was married but had figured that might not matter when it came to sleeping arrangements.

"I'm going to start working on the salad," she called to Corky and Tracy. "Maybe you two could carry over that big ice chest after you've set up your tent."

"We're almost done," said Corky as she pounded in a tent stake with a rock.

Jayne walked up to the campfire site. Adam was carefully arranging the wood. "It looks like you know what you're doing," said Jayne as she washed her hands off in a bucket of water that Harris had just carried up from the stream. "But isn't Derrick supposed to be helping you?"

"I sent him to find some more firewood." Adam grinned up at Jayne. "Just hope he doesn't get lost."

Soon Adam's fire was crackling, and Tracy and Corky were

busily wrapping potatoes in foil. Adam had set up the cooking rack for the game hens and was now trying to get a big pot of water to boil on a Coleman stove. Derrick still had not returned.

"I guess I'll go out and look for some more wood. And maybe I'll find Derrick while I'm at it," said Adam.

"He's probably off taking a nap," said Corky.

Tracy laughed. "Those coals look just about ready," she said as she threw another potato onto the quickly growing pile. "Maybe we should start putting the potatoes in."

Jayne nodded. They began to carefully drop the potatoes into the fire.

She took a deep breath. "Don't you just love days like this? Sunny and clear, but definitely fall. The smell of pine trees and wood smoke. The sound of cattle contentedly settling down for the night."

"Just like an old cowboy movie," said Corky.

Tracy sighed. "What a way to live." Then she started to sing. "The cattle are prowling, the coyotes are howling, we offer the dog a bone. Where spurs are a-jinglin', the cowboy's a-singin' this lonesome cattle call."

"That's great, Tracy," said Jayne. "Can you teach us that one? We'll be singing around the campfire tonight."

As they continued to work on dinner, Tracy taught them that song and several other cowboy tunes. After a while, Jayne noticed that Derrick returned carrying a couple of sticks of wood. She didn't say anything; so far they had exchanged only the briefest conversation, and she intended to keep it that way. Tracy started singing some songs that they all knew. Other weary, sunburned cowpokes began to trickle into camp. They all shared before-dinner snacks of crackers and cheese along with cold drinks, and as the group settled in, it seemed everyone had a good cow story to tell.

"Hey, Paul," called Harris. "Remember the time we had to keep that stray bull away from the herd?"

Paul laughed. "That's one I'd rather forget."

"Tell us," said Jayne as she put the finishing touches on the gigantic green salad.

"Well, Paul was getting pretty fed up with this old bull, so he gets his rope out and throws a loop to catch him. No problem, he ropes him just fine. We manage to hold that bull right there until the cows all get past. But then we've gotta get a move on and hurry to catch up with the herd. So I take off, and Paul's back there coiling his rope when his horse decides to take off too, at a full gallop. Well, that crazy horse heads straight for a big fir tree, ducks under a branch, and wipes Paul clean out of the saddle."

Everyone laughed.

"Poor Sarah," said Paul as he chuckled. "I was in such pain, she rubbed my back all night long."

Harris grinned. "You should've seen Paul's face when he crawled out from under that tree. I think if he'd had a gun handy he would've shot that horse."

"I sold him the next month," said Paul.

Finally dinner was ready. Once again, Jim blessed the food. Jayne sneaked a peek at Harris. She had never really heard him say much about God or religion and wondered what he thought of all this. But his hat was in his hands, and his head was bowed.

"Great meal," said Paul as they began to eat.

"Wait till you see dessert," said Corky. "Berry pies, and, believe it or not, we found ice cream buried in the bottom of the ice chest."

After dinner, Jayne went down to the creek to rinse out

some pots. Cowboy was at her heels, probably looking for more scraps. A large harvest moon was shining brightly, and she didn't even need a flashlight. One by one she rinsed the pots, with Cowboy trying to lend a helping tongue. Finally she stacked the last one into a neat pile and stooped down to rinse her hands. Next to her, Cowboy suddenly began to growl, low and deep. She reached for a cast-iron skillet, then slowly stood. The hair on her neck was standing up, and she expected to see a wild animal nearby.

"Got a minute?"

She turned in relief. It was only Derrick. Not that she was eager to see him, but he was better than a cougar. "What do you want?"

"I just want to talk."

"I don't think we have much to talk about, Derrick. I think it's better if we keep our conversations to a minimum, don't you?"

"No. And for once, Jayne, I want you to really listen to me."

"Fine, Derrick. Talk. But please get to the point."

"Will you put that pan down and sit for a minute?"

"I suppose." She set the skillet down and found a nearby rock to perch on, although everything within her was telling her to get away from him.

Derrick sat down on a rock next to her. "Jayne, I'm sorry."

This was a change. Was he really apologizing or was this a trick? "Well, like I've said already, Derrick, I forgive you." She started to stand.

"Thanks, Jayne." He reached out for her hand. "I want us back, Jayne. I want it the way it used to be—"

She pulled her hand back, but he didn't let go. Once again, Cowboy began to growl. Jayne started to stand, but Derrick blocked her way. "Derrick, I've told you over and over—"

"Jayne, just listen—"

"I don't want to listen."

"Please, Jayne. I still love you."

"Derrick, I'm sorry." She tried to pull away again, but his grip was growing tighter. She looked toward the camp, ready to scream if she had to, but reluctant to cause a big scene. "Derrick, let go of me right now, or I'll—"

"Jayne, I don't want to hurt you." He pulled her closer. She wanted to scream, but the only sound she could make was a hoarse whisper. Suddenly Cowboy began to bark wildly.

"Let go of me!" she cried as she beat her arms against him. "Leave me alone!" Cowboy was still barking, and he leaped up, trying to bite Derrick.

"Stop it right now!" yelled a voice. Jayne looked up to see Harris running toward them, with Paul on his heels. Before she knew what had happened, Harris had pulled Derrick away from her and was holding him by the shirt collar and shaking him. Jayne knelt down and clung to Cowboy.

"That's no way to treat a lady!" Harris yelled into Derrick's surprised face. Paul stepped up and took Derrick out of Harris's hands. Derrick looked relieved—until Paul punched him solidly in the stomach. Derrick came back with his fists up, but Harris grabbed him from behind and pinned his arms to his sides. By now nearly everyone from the camp had gathered around.

"I think we've had enough for tonight," said Harris through clenched teeth. "We weren't looking for a brawl, Derrick."

"That's right," said Paul as he put his face right next to Derrick's. "As much as we'd like to knock the stuffing out of you, it wouldn't be the Christian thing to do. Lucky for you I'm a different man today than I was a few years back. Now, I want you to get your things together and clear out of camp. And get off my property tonight." An uncomfortable silence followed.

Derrick's face was a mixture of anger and surprise, but it looked as if he was going to do the smart thing and leave.

Harris released Derrick roughly, and Derrick stumbled off toward camp. Jayne saw him looking at Corky, but Corky just turned away. Jayne felt sorry for Corky. She must feel nearly as bad as Jayne. Harris and Paul came over to where Jayne was now standing next to Cowboy. "Are you okay?" asked Paul as Harris wrapped a protective arm around her shoulders.

She smiled weakly. "Thanks, I'm fine. Just scared is all. It's a good thing Cowboy was here. I tried to scream, but nothing came out."

"Good job, Cowboy," said Harris, his arm still around her shoulders. It was a good feeling. Protective and comforting.

Corky and Tracy came over and gathered up the pans. "Good riddance," said Tracy.

Corky nodded, then turned to Jayne and Harris. "Sorry about that, Jayne."

"It's not your fault, Corky. But I'm sorry too," Jayne said. "But I guess we all know what he's really like now."

"Better now than after the knot was tied," said Corky. "I guess we should both be thankful to be spared."

Harris squeezed Jayne's shoulders after the others had started moving back toward camp. "Well, I bet that's the last you'll see of Derrick. Unless he's a bigger fool than I think he is."

"I would think public humiliation might do the trick for him. Just wait until the gossip mill starts churning on this one. His folks will have something to say, I'm sure, and maybe that will straighten him out. What I find hard to understand is that he calls himself a Christian. I just don't see how he could act like that."

"I've found that you can call yourself anything," said Harris, "but it's what's going on inside that makes all the difference."

160

He sat down on a rock, and Jayne sat beside him, marveling at how radically different this conversation was from the one she had just experienced. With Harris she felt safe and comfortable, and almost totally at ease.

"I don't find it very easy to talk about what I believe," said Harris in a low voice. "But the fact is, I do believe. I struggle with my faith a lot. It's sort of like a journey that I'm taking. I read the Bible and I believe in God, but I also have lots of questions. Many that haven't been answered yet. But I've tried living without God, and that was hell. I'm a lot happier knowing that God is in my life. And I know I've got a long ways to go."

Jayne smiled. "Thanks for sharing that with me, Harris. I think it sounds like you're just where you need to be. Faith is a strange thing. Sometimes I think I have it almost figured out, and then someone like Derrick comes along, professing to be this great Christian, and when things turn rotten, it blows my tiny theology to pieces. Which turned out to be a good thing in the long run—I can't believe I almost married the wrong man."

Harris leaned his head back and looked up at the stars. "So, do you think you'll know when the right one comes along?"

Jayne studied his face in the moonlight, then nodded. "I think so."

FOURTEEN

◆

The following day the weather turned cool, and a steady drizzle began to fall. Jayne could hardly stand to put a saddle on a wet horse, but Bailey accepted it without complaint. Jayne was grateful for the borrowed slicker, but after a couple of hours, the wetness had seeped down her neck and her jeans were soaked. Fortunately, the sun came out just before noon, and she began to dry and warm up again.

The rest of the cattle drive went fairly smoothly. Having Derrick gone made things go easier. Earlier that morning, Adam's horse had developed a slight limp as a result of an improperly shod hoof and had to be carefully led back to the ranch. Even with the two men gone, their group got along fine.

The horses had settled into a serious work mode. No more spooking or bucking, they got down to the business of gathering and rounding up cattle just as if they'd been doing it all their lives. They were working together like a team now, driving the tired herd to the end of the trail. Finally the last old, slow cows and young calves straggled in, and they knew their work was done. The herd was settled in the pasture at the foot of the hills, and Jayne was exhausted. She was sun baked, bug bitten, and saddle sore. All she wanted was a hot shower and then a good long soak in the tub. She didn't complain, but she almost wished they didn't have to ride back up to the ranch for the final farewell dinner. But she knew it would probably be fun, and everyone else was just as tired as she.

Paul's parents were at the ranch house when they got back,

and caterers were busily working. Everyone had eaten a light lunch in the saddle, and now they were hungry for an early dinner. Paul's dad ran a video camera, apparently with copies to be made available to those who wanted them. Jayne wasn't so sure she wanted to see herself on film after two days on horseback in the wilderness. She almost laughed when she saw her reflection in the bathroom mirror—her hair was wild, filled with pine needles, pitch, and small twigs. It would be useless to try to braid it again, so she simply pulled it back in a loose ponytail. After she washed the dust from her face she had a healthy glow to her cheeks, and she knew she could have looked worse.

By the time the food was served, the group was in high spirits. They were people who had fought a tough battle and won. Jayne was proud of how she and Bailey had helped out. They had rounded up strays, kept cattle out of the trees, and generally been a strong part of the team. Several funny and even moving speeches were made throughout the meal. She sat with Harris and Katherine, and Autumn was proudly sitting next to Paul.

"Those two have really hit it off," whispered Katherine as she nodded toward Paul at the end of the table.

"I noticed," said Jayne. "It looked as if you and Paul got along okay too."

Katherine looked down at her plate and answered quietly. "Okay, I guess."

It was the first time Jayne had ever seen Katherine caught off guard. Maybe something was brewing between her and Paul. But she respected Katherine too much to pry—at least not in public.

After the meal, horses and gear were loaded, good-byes said, and one by one they headed off, eager to get home and unload their tired animals before it got too late. After she climbed into Harris's pickup, Jayne leaned her head against the seat and sighed. "This is a comfortable cab, Harris."

"Yeah, it feels especially good after a couple days in the saddle. Go ahead and catch a few winks if you want."

Jayne closed her eyes, thinking she'd just relax a bit, but the next thing she knew they were pulling up next to Harris's barn. "Wow, I must've really zonked out."

Harris smiled. "I guess you were pretty beat."

Together they unloaded the horses and gear. Cowboy jumped down from the tailgate. "Not so peppy anymore, are you?" She picked a couple of burs off his coat. "You're a good dog, Cowboy, but you need a bath as bad as I do."

Jayne checked Bailey out from head to hoof to make sure he was okay. "You were the best horse out there, sweet thing," she said as she ran the currycomb down his back. "And don't you worry, we'll get you back into an English saddle starting tomorrow. You like that better, don't you?" His head went down, almost like a nod, and Jayne chuckled. "I thought so."

She gave him a small scoop of oats, then checked to see if the water trough was full. Harris had hired a high school boy to take care of the animals while they were gone, and everything seemed to be in good order. "Good night, sweet thing. You'll sleep well tonight."

She walked toward the house, not sure what to do next. On Friday Katherine had dropped her off, so she didn't have her car here.

"I told Katherine that I'd give you a lift home," called Harris as he walked up. "Autumn probably needs to get to bed since this is a school night."

"Thanks, Harris. I was just wondering if I should saddle Bailey and get ready for a long ride."

"Well, that would be silly. He doesn't even have headlights."

They chatted about little things that had happened on the drive as he drove her through town. It was funny how big and civilized the town suddenly seemed in contrast to having been in the wilderness for the last couple of days. Harris helped carry her things up to her apartment. As she unlocked the door, she remembered that her place was still in the same unpacked state as the last time he had seen it.

"Don't mind the boxes," she said apologetically as he set down her bag. "Can I make you some coffee or cocoa or anything?"

"Sure, some cocoa sounds good. If it's not any trouble."

Jayne smiled. "Not at all."

Harris looked around the room with a slight frown. "So, are you ever planning to unpack? Or are you thinking this is just a temporary stop?"

Jayne put two mugs of water into the microwave and began hunting for the instant cocoa. "I keep thinking I'll unpack, but then something—anything—distracts me from it. I think it's just that I can't stand it here, and by not unpacking I'm trying to convince myself I won't have to stay."

"In town, you mean?"

"No, town is okay. I just can't stand these apartments. I know it's terrible, and I should be thankful to have a roof over my head. Maybe someday I'll stop complaining and get to these boxes. Maybe when winter sets in." The microwave timer rang, and Jayne removed the two steaming cups of water, then carefully mixed in the cocoa powder. Next door she could hear the TV blaring and someone walking heavily across the floor. "See, things like that. It feels so—so unprivate and depressing. I guess my not unpacking is some sort of denial."

Harris laughed. "Maybe so."

Soon their cocoa cups were empty, and Harris stood and reached for his hat. "Thanks for the cocoa, Jayne. And thanks for all your help this weekend. Paul thinks you're quite a good horsewoman. He said to let you know you're welcome to come on his cattle drives anytime."

"Really?" Jayne stood. "That's quite a compliment, coming from Paul. How often does he do the drives?"

"Well, fall is always the big one. But he also does one in the spring. It's less of a show, and more just plain work."

"I might need some time to think about that." Jayne rubbed her backside. "Wait until I recover from this one first."

Harris laughed and then said good night.

The next week was Fire Prevention Week at school, and on Thursday, Jayne and Katherine took their classes on the bus to the fire station. When the fireman ran the siren for the children, Leah Bluefish screamed and ran into Jayne's arms. Jayne stroked her hair and told her everything was okay, but Leah didn't let go of her hand until they were back at school.

After the kids left, Jayne went into Katherine's classroom to show her an extra backpack that no one in her class had claimed. "Does this belong to anyone in your class?"

"Brent Myers," said Katherine. "He thought he left it at the fire station. Thanks. Wasn't that a fun trip today?"

"Yes, until poor Leah went hysterical."

Katherine nodded. "I heard that the tribal police were called out to her house for domestic violence this weekend."

Jayne gasped. "Is her mother okay? Did anyone get hurt?"

"I guess not. Apparently Lee has run off again. Maybe he'll stay gone for a while."

"Poor Leah."

"Yeah. It makes me think we should start making some firmer plans for our Bible Club. Autumn has been bugging me about it all week."

"Good for her. Maybe we should meet to decide some things. I've been wanting to talk to Pastor Conroy about it. I thought since he had the vision, he might have some good insights."

"Why don't you call him and set up an appointment," said Katherine as she arranged some dried gourds, corn, and small pumpkins on the science table. "Have you been invited to the Harvest Ball this weekend?"

Jayne shook her head. "No. But it sounds like fun. Have you been asked?"

Katherine laughed. "No. But that's never stopped me before. It's not really like a formal ball. Anyone can go. Lots of people go stag—it's no big deal. I just thought a certain neighbor of mine might have asked you to go."

Jayne felt her cheeks get warm. "No. We really don't have that sort of relationship, Katherine. We're good friends, that's all. Just like with you."

"You really think that's all it is?"

"I think that's all Harris wants."

"What makes you so sure?"

Jayne slumped into a child-sized chair, and like a broken dam her story poured out. "Because he hasn't said a single word to me all week. Not one word! The truth is, I almost thought we *had* reached a new level last weekend, and now this. He just walks right past me as if I wasn't even there, or as if I'm just another ranch hand—which I suppose I am in a way. But it's just so frustrating!"

Katherine laughed. "Men! Can't live with 'em—can't shoot 'em."

Jayne looked curiously at Katherine. "Actually, after last weekend, I was wondering if maybe Paul might be getting in touch with you. Perhaps he'd like to take you to the Harvest Ball...."

Katherine looked at Jayne. "Did you really think that? Why?"

"I saw him looking at you, Katherine. There was definitely some interest in his eyes. And the way he took Autumn under his wing. I don't know, but I think you'll be hearing from him before the next cattle drive."

Katherine sighed. "Well, you never know. It's fun to dream about, anyway. And Autumn thinks Paul is the greatest. But don't worry, I won't be holding my breath. I know better than to pine away over a man. In the meantime, let's go to the Harvest Ball together. We can get all dolled up and see if we turn some heads."

Jayne grinned. "That sounds like fun."

On Saturday morning, Jayne took care of the animals, then spent some time working with Bailey. She saw Harris coming and going from the barn, lingering every once in a while and looking her way. But she had decided, like Katherine, that she didn't need to pine away for a man.

Around noon, she finished up and decided to pay Jack a quick visit. She had only seen him once since the cattle drive, and they had talked mostly about the events on the drive, including Derrick's run-in with Paul and Harris. Jayne had decided that since the rumor mill in town would be running, it might as well have accurate and fresh information. As she walked toward the house, Cowboy raced out to greet her, his tail wagging faster than ever.

"Hello, Cowboy." She bent down and ran her fingers through his thick coat. "And how is my black-and-white knight in shining armor?"

"Hi there, Janie girl," called Jack. "Come on in. I've got a fresh pot of coffee on."

She sat down at the kitchen table and waited as Jack moved slowly and painfully over to her and set down a cup. "Thanks, Jack. That's just what I was wishing for. So how are you doing today?"

"Not too bad, Janie. Have you seen that son of mine around?"

She nodded. "Do you need him for something?"

"Nah, I just wondered if you'd seen him." The way Jack said it, she knew he meant another kind of seeing.

"Well, I've seen him. But I haven't actually spoken to him this week. Or rather, he hasn't spoken to me."

"Hmm. That's what I was afraid of. He's been a regular grump around the house, too. Sometimes I just don't know what gets into that boy of mine."

"Maybe he's worried about something."

Jack scratched his head. "I dunno what it could be. Everything seems to be running like clockwork around here."

"Well, I wouldn't concern myself if I were you, Jack. Harris is a grown man. He'll work it out." Jayne searched for a change of subject. "Katherine and I are going to the Harvest Ball tonight," she said brightly.

Jack smiled and looked out the window as if he was day-dreaming. "I remember the Harvest Ball. That's where I first met Jack's mother, God bless her soul. I'd just got back from Korea, been in the army. My, it was good to be home. There stood this pretty woman in a dress just about the color of a cantaloupe melon—and I hadn't had a cantaloupe melon for three years. Well, we danced together all night long. By Christmas we were engaged. Can't believe that was over forty years ago. Seems like yesterday. How I miss her."

"What a beautiful memory, Jack."

He nodded. "Sometimes memories are all an old feller like me has."

Jayne wished there were something she could do to brighten up his life. "How about coming to the dance with me and Katherine?" she asked suddenly.

Jack grinned. "Now, wouldn't that be a sight. An old coot like me with a beautiful young girl on each arm. I'd like to do it just to see the faces of some of my buddies."

"Well, why not?"

Jack rubbed his leg. "I don't know. I wouldn't be no use on the dance floor."

"That wouldn't matter. You could drink punch and watch. It might be fun. And we'll probably just end up being wallflowers anyway. We wouldn't feel quite so bad if we had a good-looking guy like you along."

"Well then, all right. I can't believe it, but you've talked me into it."

"Great. I'll tell Katherine to pick you up. I think it starts at eight."

Jayne smiled all the way home. What fun to take Jack to the dance. It would be a night to remember. Fortunately Katherine was of the same mind when she called and told her about it. Katherine invited Jayne to come to her house to get ready. Her cousin, Kara, was a beautician and could help them do their hair. Then Kara would stay with Autumn for the evening.

Jayne couldn't decide what to wear. Katherine said they were going all out, but Jayne wasn't sure what that meant. She had about three dresses that seemed to qualify. One was a simple black silk that, while not flashy, was appropriate for most occasions. Then she had a full-skirted dress in earth tones that looked like it would be fun to dance in. Her last choice was a sapphire blue sequined number that she had worn to a college dance her sophomore year. It was definitely flashy. She decided to take all three to Katherine's.

"You have to wear the blue one," said Autumn as soon as Jayne showed the three dresses.

Jayne made a face. "I don't know. It's pretty wild."

Katherine giggled. "Well, I've got one that's probably even wilder." She left the room and quickly returned with a red sequined dress very similar to Jayne's.

"Oh, you'll both look like princesses," said Autumn as she fingered her mother's dress.

When Kara arrived, she agreed with Autumn, and it was decided that for tonight, sequins ruled. Before long, both Katherine and Jayne had their tresses piled high and were adorned in cubic zirconia that glittered like diamonds.

"I feel like we're playing dress-up," said Jayne.

"I know, but you have to admit it's fun," said Katherine as they stood before the bathroom mirror. "And Jack will love it."

"I hope we don't give him a heart attack," said Jayne. "And to think just last week we were covered with trail dust and smelled like livestock."

They both went up to the house to pick up Jack. To Jayne's amazement, Harris opened the door. He had on a dirty white T-shirt and dusty Wranglers, and his mouth literally dropped open. "What the—"

"Didn't Jack tell you that we're taking him to the Harvest Ball?" Katherine said politely as she stepped into the living room. Jayne followed, stifling giggles. She felt as if she were in junior high, pulling a joke on a boyfriend.

Just then, Cowboy came up and cautiously sniffed them, unsure of what was going on. But when he realized it was Jayne, he began to dance around like a little black-and-white jester. Harris was still shaking his head in amazement. He stared at Jayne as if she were a stranger.

"The Harvest Ball?" he finally said lamely. "Dad is going—"

"That's right, son," Jack said as he stepped into the room. "At least one of the McAllister men is still interested in having a good time." He was wearing an old but neatly pressed pin-striped suit with a crisp white shirt and tie. Suddenly he stopped in his tracks and stared at the two women. "Why, ladies, you two look just like movie starlets. Are you really taking me to the ball?"

Jayne took his arm. "That's right, Jack. And you look stunning. We'll be the talk of the town." She turned to Harris and smiled brightly. "Now, don't worry, Harris, we'll take good care of him. And you have a nice evening."

The three of them laughed all the way to the car. And Jayne was right; at the Harvest Ball almost all eyes were on them. People from all walks of life came up to chat with the strange threesome. Before long, Jayne and Katherine were getting invitations to dance. They took turns sitting with Jack, but with as many people as Jack knew, they weren't worried that he would be bored. In fact, he seemed to be having the time of his life. He even said his arthritis wasn't bothering him.

An hour into the evening, Jayne and Katherine went to pick up some refreshments for their table. "Aren't the decorations sweet?" said Jayne as she admired the bare tree branches with tiny white lights strung through them. Cornstalks, Indian corn, and pumpkins were arranged along the outer walls. Some of the old-timers were sitting on straw bales, looking on with amusement.

"Look at the food," said Katherine. "They've really outdone themselves this year." There were elaborately arranged trays of meat and cheese, spice cakes, pumpkin and apple pies, hot spiced cider, and an array of hot dishes. They filled their own plates and one for Jack, then returned to their table.

A western band was playing, and naturally, old cowboy tunes dominated, but there were a few contemporary songs and classics mixed in for good measure. About midway through one dance, Jayne was out on the floor with Paul's younger brother, Adam Roderick, when she saw a familiar figure enter the room and look around. It was Harris, all cleaned up and wearing a suit. Jayne politely tried to concentrate on Adam through the duration of the dance, but the whole while she was wondering what had brought Harris out tonight. Was he worried about his dad? Or was it something more? Finally, the song ended and she thanked Adam and made her way back to where Jack was stationed. Theirs had been one of the more popular tables of the evening.

"Hi Harris," she said lightly as she came to the table. "We didn't know you were coming tonight."

Jack chuckled. "Just couldn't stand to see the old man having all the fun, could you, son?"

Harris smiled. "I guess not. Can I join you folks, or is this a private party?"

"By all means, join us," said Jayne. She felt Harris's eyes on her flashy dress and wanted to sit down and try to hide, at least partially, behind the table. The band struck up a new song, and the lead singer started singing "El Paso." This favorite romantic tune had several couples already heading for the dance floor.

"It's my turn to dance," announced Katherine as John Gray, a single teacher from their school, came over to them. "But since Harris is here, I guess he can sit with Jack while we dance." She winked at Jayne. Harris frowned.

Jack just laughed. "I haven't had any problem keeping this table full." He turned to old Howard Gunderson and grinned. "Right, Howie?"

"In that case, maybe Jayne would like to dance," said Harris. She wasn't sure if he was talking to her or his dad. Did he mean that he wanted to dance with her, or was he sending her away? "So do you?" he asked.

"What?" She looked at him with innocent eyes, as if she hadn't heard him the first time.

"Do you want to dance?"

"With you?"

"Y-yes," he stammered. "That's what I had in mind."

"I'd love to." She smiled sweetly.

Harris smiled back and stood. He took her hand and looked at her again for another long moment, then guided her out to the dance floor. She glanced at his charcoal gray suit as they walked. It didn't look very new, but was a fairly classic style and didn't seem too dated. Out on the floor, she turned and faced him. Although she had on very high heels, he was still a little bit taller. But with the added height she was almost able to look straight into his eyes. And what she thought she saw there took her breath away.

It was one of those moments when it felt as though life were changing, shifting directions, whether she was ready or not. When Harris took her in his arms, she wondered if he could feel her heart pounding. Maybe this was a bad idea. Suddenly she felt like butter on a hot day. She had never been this close to Harris before. And she had never felt quite like this with Derrick—or with any other man for that matter. What was happening here? Could Harris feel it too, or was it just her?

By the third dance, she had managed to calm her heart down a little. But at the same time, she never wanted this night to end. It was as if something had clicked in her, and now she wanted to dance in his arms forever. But it was disturbing to feel so vulnerable. When the music stopped, Harris kept hold of one hand and they returned to the table without saying a word. Jayne looked down at Jack. He was smiling brightly up at them, but she could tell that he was tiring.

"How are you doing, Jack?" she asked as they sat down.

"Okay, I guess. It's sure been fun. But I guess I'm starting to feel like Cinderfella." He pointed to a pumpkin over by the harvest decorations. "I might turn into one of those if I don't get home soon."

Harris looked at Jayne, then back to his father. "I'll take you home, Dad."

"Oh, son, I hate to spoil your evening—"

"You aren't, Dad. Actually, I'm kind of tired too." He turned to Jayne. "Do you and Katherine mind if I take your date home?"

"Not at all." She turned to Jack. "It was great of you to come with us. It was such fun."

Jack smiled. "It surely was, Janie girl. You tell Katherine thank you for me."

"I will, Jack." She stood and took his hand. "I feel honored to have spent my first Harvest Ball in the company of—" she paused, glancing over at Harris—"two fine McAllister men."

Harris grinned. "Thanks, Jayne. See you around. I don't imagine you two girls will be staying out too late. Don't you have church in the morning?" His blue eyes glinted slightly, as if suggesting that she get herself home.

"Well, as a matter of fact, we do. But the night is still young, and I don't think Katherine is ready to go just yet."

"Take care of yourself, Jayne," he said quietly. "You're looking way too good to be out in public without an escort."

"Thank you for the compliment," she said, then she turned and walked toward the refreshment table. She felt his eyes on her with every step she took and thought it was nice to have the upper hand for a change. But suddenly she remembered how she felt in his hands. Maybe she didn't want the upper hand after all.

FIFTEEN

◆

T he date for the first Bible Club meeting was set for the first Saturday in November. Pastor Conroy had given them encouragement, some funds to get started, and a few names of families who might be interested. Autumn made colorful flyers to hang at the reservation store and several of the schools where tribal children attended. On Saturday, only six kids showed up at Katherine's house, counting Autumn. But that was exactly what Pastor Conroy had predicted, so Jayne and Katherine tried to mask their disappointment and launched right into the craft session, snack time, activity, and finally the Bible story. The whole session was only two hours, but by the time they were done it seemed as if it had lasted much longer.

"Teaching kindergarten is a lot easier than this," said Jayne as they packed up the craft supplies and washed glue from Katherine's kitchen table.

"I know. But I thought it would be tough to start with."

"I think everyone had fun," said Autumn brightly.

"Really?" asked Jayne.

"Yes, and Jonathan Two Feather said he's bringing a friend next week."

"See," said Katherine. "This is how these things start. It reminds me of a Scripture. I can't remember exactly where it is, but it says something like, 'don't despise small beginnings.'"

"Okay. Maybe that should be our motto," said Jayne as she looked at one of the nature wall hangings they had made for the craft project. She held it up to the light so that the fall leaves looked even more colorful. "We have to start somewhere."

By the third Saturday, the group had almost tripled in size to a total of twenty-three kids, and the two hours flew by. Afterwards, a girl named Rose stayed late and asked Katherine and Jayne to pray with her. When they finished praying, Rose's dark eyes shone and she politely thanked them both. Jayne couldn't remember when she had ever felt so happy.

"Next week," Katherine promised Rose, "we'll have a Bible for you." Autumn walked Rose out to the porch, chattering excitedly about how Rose might enjoy coming to Sunday school with them the next day. And Rose agreed.

"Isn't it great?" said Katherine. "But I'm afraid they're outgrowing my house. I wonder where we could go to have more room. The tribe has a big meeting room, but I doubt if the council will let us use it."

"What about Harris's barn? There's that big wood stove in there. If we cranked it up, it might be warm enough. And the kids could probably sit on the hay bales."

"It might work, unless it got too cold. But maybe we could think of something else then. Will you ask Harris?"

Jayne frowned. "I suppose I could. At least it would be a way to initiate a conversation with him."

"Is he being cool and aloof again?"

Jayne nodded. "I'm starting to feel like a yo-yo."

Katherine laughed. "Well, I really think the problem is whenever Harris feels drawn to you, it scares him. He's afraid to get his heart involved and risk getting hurt again. So he gets all defensive and gives you a big push away. I bet you do feel like a yo-yo. But if you can just be a patient yo-yo, I think things will turn out all right."

"A patient yo-yo." She grinned. "Now that's a beautiful metaphor."

"Harris is a good man, Jayne. There aren't many people I respect more than him. But it's going to take some time for him to work this thing out. Just hang in there."

"I don't think I have a choice."

Katherine looked at her with raised brows. "Something you haven't told me?"

Jayne tried not to smile. "I tell you this in the strictest confidence."

"These lips are sealed."

"Something happened inside me at the Harvest Ball. It seems silly to say it out loud, but I'm pretty sure that I've fallen in love with the man—may God help me."

Katherine squeezed her hand. "That's great, Jayne. I wasn't going to tell you this, since you and Harris are such good friends, but I've never seen Harris look at anyone the way he looks at you. Now, that's all I'm going to say."

"Thanks."

"Now, do you have any plans for Thanksgiving next week?"

"No. I don't really want to go to my parents' house. They're going to have dinner with some friends, and I don't think they'll miss me. Plus, I was looking forward to getting some nice long rides on Bailey with the extra time off."

"How about helping me host a dinner at my place on Thursday? Autumn has asked if we could do a *real* Thanksgiving dinner. As you can imagine, it's not a normal Native American tradition around here, but I need to remember to honor Autumn's heritage too. Sometimes I almost forget about her other half."

"Well, I'd be glad to help."

"I thought we'd invite Jack and Harris and my mom.

Autumn wants to invite my uncle, which will surely make things interesting. I'm not sure who else; maybe that's enough. It will be an old-fashioned gathering of the white folks and Indians." Katherine smiled coyly. "Hopefully my uncle won't want to go on the warpath."

"Well, it sounds like it could be interesting. I wouldn't want to miss it. Just tell me what to bring and do, and I'll be there."

During Thanksgiving week, Jayne did all kinds of fun activities with her class. She used the holiday as the basis of lessons to teach the children to show respect and honor to Native Americans. By the time they had their little feast on Wednesday, the children seemed to be thinking it was pretty cool to be Native American. Even Leah was holding her head up higher.

On Thursday morning, Jayne rose early. She had made two pumpkin pies, which were now sitting in the refrigerator. They were the first she'd ever made, but they looked pretty good. She glanced around her living room. During the last few days, she had finally begun to unpack. As she taught the children about how the Native Americans and pilgrims lived, she had begun to feel a little guilty for not appreciating her own home, however meager it seemed. Now she was almost finished putting things away, and her place didn't look too bad. She had even hung some pictures on the walls and arranged some dried flowers in a stoneware pot that Katherine had made for her. She set the arrangement on the antique sewing machine that her grandmother had given her. Maybe the next time Harris was here, if there was a next time, he would see that she was settling in.

Katherine seemed to have everything under control when

she arrived, and she put Jayne to work peeling potatoes.

"We're having a little bit of everything," explained Katherine. "Autumn insisted on a turkey, but I'm also cooking a venison roast. My mom is bringing some fry bread and her homemade huckleberry jam."

"Sounds good to me." Jayne dropped a peeled potato into the pot of water. "How many are we expecting?"

"Well, there's my mom and Uncle John, or Black Hawk, as he prefers to be called. And of course, Jack and Harris. I also invited Mary and Leah Bluefish. Lee still hasn't returned, and I saw Mary at the grocery store yesterday, and the next thing I knew I was asking her and Leah to come, and she said yes."

"Good for you."

"I hope so. I just don't want Uncle John to make any scenes today. It was important for Autumn to have him come, but sometimes the man absolutely delights in being contrary."

"Sounds like fun."

Katherine groaned. "You must have a twisted idea of what fun is."

Jayne laughed. "Maybe. But it should at least be interesting."

Harris and Jack arrived at two o'clock, just as Katherine had said, but everyone else was late. "This is typical," explained Katherine. "They have their own sense of time."

"It's all right, Katherine," said Jack as he settled onto the couch. "We've been living on the reservation long enough to understand that. In fact, I remember the time I hired the Thistle Tree brothers to put up a fence on the back forty. I hired them in spring, thinking they'd be done by fall, and that was allowing plenty of time. But they didn't finish up until the next spring, and that was with me threatening to finish it myself."

Katherine laughed. "I suppose I'd be just like that if I hadn't gone off to college and taken a job in the real world.

Sometimes I wonder who's smarter, though, especially on Monday mornings in the dead of winter when it's cold and dark outside."

"You and me both," said Jayne. "I don't think you have to be Native American to wonder about that."

"But you wouldn't be able to live like that all the time," said Harris.

Just then a dilapidated Buick pulled in front of Katherine's house, parking on the lawn right in front of the porch. Katherine's eyes flashed, but she didn't mention the strange parking place. Instead she smiled and opened the door.

"Hello," she called.

"Hello, Katherine," said Joanne as she pulled her stout body out of the low car. "We gave Mary and Leah a ride too."

Greetings and introductions were made, and soon everyone was seated around the two tables that Katherine and Jayne had pushed together. Katherine told everyone how glad she was that they could come, and then asked Jack to say a blessing.

Conversation didn't flow easily during the meal. Katherine tried several times, and then Jayne gave it a shot.

"I certainly enjoy having Leah in my classroom," she said to Mary. "She's a bright little girl."

Mary smiled. "She is smart, I think. She draws good pictures, too."

"Yes, I've seen her do some beautiful pictures at school."

"She likes to go to school. I think you are a good teacher."

"Thank you. I've sure enjoyed—"

Black Hawk cut her off. "Indian children should have a reservation school," he said bluntly.

"Why do you think that?" Jayne asked, although she wasn't sure it was wise to pursue this topic.

"It's no good for them to learn white man's ways. They are

forgetting about their people, their traditions, their language."

"Don't they learn those things on the reservation?"

"No, they spend all their time going to white man's school. Soon they will think your ways are better than ours."

Jayne turned to Mary. "Did you go to public school?"

Mary nodded silently. She didn't look as if she wanted to be included in the conversation.

"And did you forget about your people and their traditions?"

Mary shook her head, not allowing her eyes to go to where Black Hawk was seated across from them.

Black Hawk glanced at Katherine. "But look at Katherine. She ran off to college and now teaches in a white man's school."

"Why must you call it a white man's school, Uncle?" asked Katherine. "All sorts of children go there, and look at me—am I white?"

"Almost." Black Hawk turned back to Jayne. "Why are you so interested in our people anyway? Why have you come here?"

Jayne blinked in surprise. "Why, uh, I came here to teach. And Katherine is my best friend. I don't think of her as Native American—I just think of her as Katherine."

Black Hawk pointed with his knife. "See, you don't think of her as Indian, because she lives like a white woman—"

"And exactly how does a white woman live?" asked Katherine, her dark eyes angry. Jayne felt guilty for not trying to steer the conversation another way. Everyone at the table was sitting quietly. No one was eating.

Black Hawk laughed. "Look around your house, and you will see."

"Well, John," said Joanne, "I think my daughter's house is very nice."

"If you ask me," said Jack, "there are all kinds of white women, and I don't think I've ever seen two just alike. I think the same goes with Indians."

Jayne smiled. "Yes, in fact, until this week I was living like a vagrant myself. My apartment was full of cardboard boxes, but I finally decided to unpack."

"Good for you, Jayne," said Katherine. "See, we are all different. Vive la différence!"

"There you go, talking in white man words," said Black Hawk.

"It's French, Uncle. And you know good and well that I also speak my mother tongue fluently. Now let's quit arguing."

The rest of dinner proceeded without conflict. Jack told an old hunting story, and Black Hawk told a story to top it. Fortunately, Jack knew better than to try to one-up Black Hawk. Finally, it looked as if everyone had eaten as much as they wanted.

"Why don't you all go into the living room?" said Jayne. She looked at Katherine. "You can enjoy a little break while I clear the table. And no arguing."

"Okay," said Katherine. "We'll relax a bit, then have some dessert. Maybe Autumn would like to show Leah her room." Autumn agreed, taking Leah by the hand as the adults moved into the living room.

Jayne listened to the conversation as she cleared the table. Joanne asked how the booth in the crafter's mall was doing, and Katherine filled her in on the details. Jayne knew that Joanne was enjoying having a little extra spending money each month. Harris was asking Black Hawk about how hunting had been lately, mentioning that he had failed to get an elk tag this year and how he missed it.

Black Hawk laughed. "Poor white men, you have to sign up and register for everything. We just go out and hunt whenever we like."

"Doesn't seem fair, does it," said Harris. His voice sounded stiff, as if he really wanted to say more but was keeping himself in check.

"Considering what the white man did to my people, I do not worry about what seems fair. The white man did not care about what was fair for my people. Fair does not exist."

"I agree with you about some of that, but is it right that people like me get blamed for what happened long before we were born?"

"You would be no different. Look at you now; you are no different. You take our land, you fence it off, you build barns and buildings all over it—"

"Wait a minute! First of all, I didn't take anyone's land. Dad bought it from your own council over thirty years ago—"

"That was a foolish council—"

"Dessert, anyone?" asked Jayne. "Harris, could you give me a hand in here? I want to let Katherine have a break."

"Sure, I'd be happy to." Harris excused himself and came into the kitchen.

"How about making some coffee," said Jayne loud enough for the others to hear.

"Thanks for rescuing me," he whispered. "It was getting a little too hot in there."

Jayne nodded. "Poor Katherine. It sounds like he's going after her now."

"Maybe we should ask her to come help too," Harris said as he filled the coffeepot with water.

"Say, Harris," said Jayne as she sliced a pumpkin pie,

"Katherine and I are having this Bible Club at her house, but last week there were twenty-three kids here and it was pretty packed."

"Reservation kids?"

"Yes. And we were wondering where we might have it if the numbers continue to increase. I thought about your barn. You have that wood stove in there, and the kids could sit on hay bales—"

"Reservation kids in my barn?"

"Yeah. Is something wrong with that?"

"I don't know, Jayne."

"Why not?"

"It feels like you're stepping over the line here. I mean, listen to Black Hawk. People like him won't think kindly of someone like me—a white man who lives on the reservation—having a bunch of Indian kids meet in his barn for some Bible Club."

"Are you afraid?"

Harris shook his head. "No. It doesn't have to do with fear. It's just common sense. It puts me in an awkward position."

"I see." Jayne turned and began putting pie slices onto plates. She didn't know why he was being so stubborn about this. Didn't he care about the kids?

"Need any more help?" asked Katherine. In a quieter voice she added, "I had to get away before I threw something at my uncle. But we probably shouldn't leave Jack in there; he may be the next victim."

"I'll go back," said Harris as he switched on the coffeepot. Jayne figured he thought her as bad as Black Hawk—maybe worse. She continued quietly dishing out the pie, not wanting to tell Katherine about Harris's response to her request. She had been so sure he would agree.

At last dessert was over. Jayne thanked Katherine for everything, then pleaded a headache, which was true, and excused herself. She wanted to get away from there. Or maybe it was just away from Harris. For some reason she felt personally offended when he didn't agree to let them have Bible Club in his barn.

On the way home, she prayed that God would provide the perfect place, or else keep their numbers within reason until they had more room. It was futile to fret over it. And perhaps it was a way of showing her that she didn't know Harris as well as she thought she did. She remembered that she had once thought she'd known Derrick. There was a time when she'd been convinced he would make a wonderful husband. It was quite possible to be wrong more than once.

Sixteen

◆

"Miss Morgan?"

Jayne waved good-bye to the last stragglers in her class, then turned to see a man who looked somewhat familiar. He was shorter than she and dressed in typical cowboy attire—western shirt, Wrangler jeans, scuffed boots, and a belt with an oversized silver buckle. Finally, she remembered—Rebecca's father.

"Mr. Howard. How are you?"

"I'm all right, I guess. Last week, Rebecca came home and told us about how you've been teaching a lot of stuff about Indians."

"That's right. Since last week was Thanksgiving we spent some time learning about Native Americans and how they helped the pilgrims to settle in the New World. It's really a wonderful way to celebrate the friendship between two different cultures."

"Don't you go wasting your city-talk and expensive words on me, Miss Morgan. We don't call them Native Americans around here. Now, I'm an American, and maybe you're an American, but they are called Indians. Plain and simple—Indians. Do you get it?"

Jayne stared at him.

"And furthermore, young lady, it's folks like me that financially support every single thing the Indians do. Did you know that? We taxpayers, we get stuck with the bill. The Indians get to live on free land, in free houses, and get money for doing absolutely nothing. And we pay for it."

"I don't understand what this—"

"Let me finish! I don't work all day just to spend my hard-earned tax dollars to support them Indians, and then to support this public school just so liberal-minded teachers like you can come in here and 'celebrate diversity.' I send Rebecca to school to learn to read and write, not to use fancy words like *Native American* and whatever else you've put into her head. And I'm not alone in this. There's plenty more that agree with me. If I had it my way those Indian kids would have school on the reservation. If they don't want to come out here and live like we do, then they can just teach their own kids."

"You sound as if you hate them." Jayne looked into the man's eyes, trying to understand where these deep-rooted feelings came from.

He folded his arms against his chest and leaned back slightly. "No, it's not like I hate them. But we have a way of life in this town." His voice grew slightly softer, as if he were explaining something to his five-year-old daughter. "You're a newcomer here, so maybe you don't understand. But there are some unspoken rules around here. For instance, we all know that the Indians can't help what they are, and for the most part we just try and let them be. Sure, it irks us sometimes that they've got it so easy, especially when some of us are struggling just to pay the rent and keep food on the table."

"It doesn't seem like you understand them very well."

"Who doesn't understand who? You're the newcomer in this town. I've lived here all my life. You think I don't understand them?"

Jayne nodded. "Maybe that's the problem. You've lived here all your life, and you've heard things, and believed things, but maybe you don't really know what's true. For instance, one of my best friends is Native American—"

"There you go again calling 'em Native Americans. They're just Indians. If anything, I should be called a Native American. I was born here too!"

"All right, for this conversation, I'll call them Indians. My friend has been to college; she's one of the most intelligent women I know. She's creative and talented. She has respect for both the white world and her own—"

"I know you're talking about Katherine Patawa. She's different. But even Katherine has a hard time with the Indians. They didn't accept her at first when she came back here to teach. She lived in a different world. They didn't like that. You see, they just need to stay in their own little world and we need to stay in ours."

"And that would make the world a better place?"

"That's right!"

"I don't know about you, Mr. Howard, but my great-grandpa came over here on a boat from Europe. He was Italian, and some people in this country didn't like that. Then he came by covered wagon over to the West Coast. He was a foreigner. You must realize that America is made of many different kinds of people, from different countries, different cultures—a melting pot. It hasn't been easy for people to get along, but all things considered, it's worked out pretty well. You may recall that we fought a war so that African Americans could be freed from slavery and later win the right to vote and be equal. And we fought another war to protect Jewish people from Hitler's persecution—"

"Am I getting a history lesson here?"

"Maybe you need it."

"The only thing I need is for you to start acting like a teacher, and not some left-wing liberal radical who thinks she's going to teach my daughter how to pound a tom-tom and string beads."

"Like it or not, Mr. Howard," she said, her voice raised, "Native American culture is part of our American history. And I will teach it!"

"You do what you think best, Miss Morgan, but you haven't heard the last of me."

"I didn't think I had. And I'm sorry you feel this way."

Jayne struggled to regain her control. She didn't like to think that she had actually yelled at a parent. But she couldn't remember when she had met such an aggravating man. He made Black Hawk seem like a pussycat. She wondered what would happen if they locked Black Hawk and Mr. Howard up in a room together.

After Mr. Howard left, she quickly finished cleaning her classroom, washing out the paintbrushes and picking up a few stray blocks. She wondered if Mr. Howard would really have any influence. Would the school board even give him the time of day? She couldn't imagine anyone with any intelligence taking him seriously. She had only attempted to discuss the matter in hopes of persuading him to see his Native American neighbors in a new light. Part of her wanted to run to Katherine and pour out the horrible story, but another part of her wanted to protect her friend from hearing about the outright bigotry of people like Mr. Howard. For now the best thing was probably just to pray about it and put it out of her mind.

Riding Bailey always proved a good distraction to most problems. As she galloped him across the field later that afternoon, she felt free and light again. The air blew crisp and cold against her face, and she wrapped her scarf more tightly around her neck. Winter was just around the corner. She had only been riding for about an hour, but already the sun was dipping low into the western sky. It was a clear day, and the sky stretched on and on in a pale shade of blue. It was amazing how the sky changed here. She had seen it turn every color of the rainbow. And there was just so much of it.

She thought about how all the people in the world shared the same sky. The world was kind of like a beautiful quilt designed and stitched by God. He'd created all the people in it, not differentiating between color or culture, rich or poor, plain or beautiful. Why couldn't everyone think of different cultures that way?

Those thoughts were running through her head as she rode Bailey back toward the barn. She thought of the Bible Club kids again. The numbers had stayed solid last Saturday, and she and Katherine were seriously looking for another location. At least these kids would hear that all were equal, and that God loved everyone. And as for the children in her kindergarten class, it would take more than the likes of Mr. Howard to shut her up.

"Everything okay?" asked Harris as she dismounted.

She jumped, unaware that he was in the barn. "I guess so," she answered without much enthusiasm.

"That doesn't sound very convincing."

Jayne didn't answer. After her last talk with him in Katherine's kitchen, she felt cautious with him. She was no longer sure exactly who he was. She was afraid she had turned him into someone entirely different in her mind.

He stepped up and took off his work gloves. "Jayne? Are you okay?"

She nodded. "Yeah, I'm fine. Just tired, I guess. It's been a long day." She hoped he would take that as a hint that she wanted to unsaddle Bailey and be on her way.

But he didn't step away. "I've been wanting to talk to you. I spoke to Dad about you and Katherine wanting to use the barn. I think I might have overreacted. Dad couldn't see that it would be any problem, and after I thought about it, neither did I."

"Really?"

"Really. And I'm sorry if I acted like a jerk about it." He nodded to the barn. "See, I've even been cleaning it up a little. Trying to make sure that it's a safe place for kids."

She wanted to hug him, but held herself back. "Thanks, Harris. You don't know how good that makes me feel, especially after—" She stopped.

"After what?"

"Oh, it was probably nothing. Just a little scene at school."

"Do you want to talk about it?"

She shrugged and looked at her horse. "I don't know. I need to get Bailey's saddle off and brush him and then let him dry. I ran him pretty hard out there."

Harris rolled his eyes. "He's just a horse, Jayne. He'll be fine. Just take off his saddle and let him be."

"I can't."

"What do you mean, you can't?"

"Because he's my friend." Suddenly and unexpectedly, tears came. She turned away. "And I've had a rough day."

He put his hand on her shoulder. "I'm sorry, Jayne. I didn't mean to upset you. It's hard for me to understand the way you treat that animal. But it's okay." Harris's voice was low and soothing. It was comforting, but it also made her feel even more ridiculous. She wiped her nose on her sleeve, and then he handed her a handkerchief.

"Thanks. I don't know what's wrong with me."

"It's okay. I can come on pretty hard sometimes. I guess it

comes with being a crusty old bachelor. Even Dad tells me to watch it."

"I just had kind of a bad day. Actually, the day was okay, but a parent came in and—" Tears threatened again.

"Jayne, let me help you with the saddle, then I'll take you out for a steak. That always makes me feel better."

"I don't really like steak."

"You don't like steak?" Harris scratched his chin. "But the other time we went out, you had a steak."

"I know. That's because you did."

Harris laughed. "Well, you don't have to have steak. You can have whatever you want."

"Really?"

"Yes." He gave her a gentle shove. "Now go sit down while I take care of your horse."

They ended up going for hamburgers, which suited Jayne just fine. Her unexpected crying jag had ended, and even though she still felt silly and self-conscious, she was thankful for Harris's concern. It was encouraging.

She took another sip of the chocolate shake and continued telling him the story of Mr. Howard. "I tried to reason with him. I even reminded him of how we freed the blacks from slavery and fought for the Jews."

Harris laughed. "I would have loved to have seen his face."

"He didn't even seem to listen."

"You're fighting an uphill battle, Jayne. The dividing lines here are old and deep."

"Do you feel like that about Native—I mean, Indians, as you call them?"

"Well, we do call them Indians. They call themselves Indians. No one seems to mind."

"But in college—"

"This isn't college, Jayne. It's a different world here, like it or not. Maybe some things will change, but it will take a lot of time and work."

Jayne nodded. "Do you really think things will change?"

"I don't know. What you and Katherine are doing with that Bible Club could make a difference. But you have to be patient and not push things."

"You think I push things?"

"A little."

Jayne looked down at her unfinished French fries. "It's just so hard to stand back and watch people live with such divisions, such bigotry."

"Maybe they like to live that way."

She looked into his eyes. He was totally serious. "You think they're happy?"

"Maybe not exactly happy. But they might be content to leave things as they are. Is that so bad?"

She shook her head. "I don't know. I feel so confused. I just don't know anymore."

"I don't know what to tell you, Jayne. But I do remember something my mom used to say when I was a kid."

Jayne looked up at him. He had never said anything about his mother before. "What did she say?"

He swallowed. "Well, sometimes, like if I was having a hard time doing the right thing or getting into trouble, Mom would look me in the eyes and say, 'I don't expect you to know all the answers, Harris, but I want you to listen to your heart. Just listen to your heart.'" He looked away. Jayne wasn't sure, but she thought his eyes were misty. She wanted to reach out to him, but instead kept her hands in her lap.

"That's good advice, Harris." He looked back at her and she

smiled. "Thanks for sharing that with me. I think that's exactly what I needed to hear."

Harris paid the bill, and they went outside and stood under the streetlights. She thanked him for dinner, then neither of them said anything. They just stood there silently for a long moment. She had driven her car into town to save an unnecessary trip, but now she wished she hadn't. She wouldn't have minded spending some extra time with him. Instead they parted and went their separate ways. But just the same, she felt encouraged. And whether or not it was true, she felt loved.

SEVENTEEN

I'm so glad that Harris decided to let us use his barn for Bible Club," said Katherine as they set up the craft project on card tables. "It's not only convenient, but it makes for a pretty fun setting. I think the kids will like it."

"Maybe we could bring a Christmas tree in," said Jayne. "We could decorate it and explain what some of the symbols of Christmas mean."

"That would be fun!" said Autumn. "I bet the kids would like that." With her mother's artistic flair, she had draped a tablecloth over a bale of hay and was arranging the snacks on top.

Soon the kids began to arrive. Pastor Conroy and a couple of others from church had volunteered to drive their vans to bring kids back and forth from Bible Club. They had designated several pickup spots on the reservation for kids who needed rides, and it was a sure way to get the kids there on time.

After several ice-breaker games, Jayne led a craft session, making quilts from red and green construction paper to be used as Christmas ornaments. She announced to the children that next week they would have a tree to decorate. After that, they had refreshments served by Autumn. Every week, they learned a new Bible verse, and during snack time, prizes were given to those who could remember the verses from the previous weeks. After another game and a few songs, Katherine told a dramatized story about when Jesus was born on earth. She was a natural storyteller, and the children listened attentively to every word. After the story, Rose raised her hand.

"I read about some people who dressed up like Mary and Joseph and the shepherds and everything, and they got real animals and a manger and set it up at a church for Christmas."

"You mean a live nativity," said Jayne. "I've seen them before, and they look really cool. It makes you feel like you've gone back in time."

"Could we do that?" asked Rose.

"Yeah," chimed in several others.

Katherine looked at Jayne, then back at Rose. "You mean here in the barn?"

"No," said Rose. "I mean for everyone. Maybe we could do it in town."

"In town?" said Katherine, tossing a questioning look at Jayne.

"Maybe in front of the church?" said Jayne.

"Yeah," said Autumn. "Pastor Conroy would let us do it there."

Soon everyone was talking at once. Some were asking to be angels. Others were offering to bring animals. It was starting to feel like a circus.

"Quiet down," said Jayne. "Listen, everyone, if we really want to do this, we'll have to be organized. But I think it can be done. Maybe what we should do is dedicate our next meeting to planning exactly what we'll do and actually practice a little. We don't have much time to pull this off, but I think we can do it. It would probably help if everyone looked at home for things that might work for clothing. We'll need stuff like bathrobes, blankets, sheets. And if you have an animal that might work, like goats or sheep or donkeys—"

"Should we bring the animals next week?" asked a boy. "We have an old mule."

"No," said Jayne, laughing. "Let's not bring the animals. We'll just make a list of who has what animals and put together a plan for getting them to the nativity. We'll have to talk about dates and times, and we'll need to put something together for a stable and manger."

"I know how to build things," said a tall boy named Sam who had never said a word before.

"Good," said Katherine. "Maybe you could be in charge of the building projects." Several other boys immediately offered to help him.

"Well," said Jayne, looking at her watch, "we've already gone past quitting time. I'm sure your rides are waiting outside." The kids groaned.

"Don't forget to practice your Bible verse," said Katherine. "We'll see everyone next week."

They walked the kids out to the driveway where the vans were waiting. Everyone was still chattering with excitement. Jayne went up to the van that Pastor Conroy was driving.

"Looks like Bible Club is a huge success," said Pastor Conroy. "These kids don't want to leave."

Jayne smiled. "Well, that's because we just came up with a great idea. But we'll need your help."

"What is it?"

"The kids would like to do a live nativity for Christmas. We were wondering if we could have it at your church?"

Pastor Conroy scratched his chin. "Sure, that would be okay. But I wonder if there might be a better location, a place where more people could see it. Maybe the city park?"

"Do you think they would let us?"

"The mayor happens to be a good friend of mine. I could certainly ask."

"Oh, Pastor Conroy, that would be great. It could be a real event!"

Jayne and Katherine waved good-bye as the vans pulled out. Then Jayne told Katherine about Pastor Conroy's idea.

"That would be nice," said Katherine. "As long as it doesn't turn into a problem."

"What do you mean?"

"Oh, you know how people can be. They might think it was some sort of a political thing. And you know how a lot of folks think about Indians and all. I just wouldn't want to see the kids get hurt because the adults started acting childish."

Jayne remembered Mr. Howard. She could just imagine what someone like him would think of the Indian kids doing a religious production in the city park. "Maybe you're right, Katherine. Maybe we should ask Pastor Conroy to rethink this."

"Or maybe we should just pray about it and ask God to control the situation."

Katherine called Autumn over and the three of them went into the barn and quietly prayed about the live nativity, putting the whole thing into God's hands.

During the next week, Jayne and Katherine tried to gather as many things as they could find to use as props and costumes for the live nativity. Even Jack was getting into the production. He donated some old costume jewelry and a pair of golden shoes that had belonged to his late wife.

"She would be happy to see these things used for this," said Jack as he reverently handed the items to Jayne. "She was always trying to reach out to the children who lived on the reservation. It would please her to know that you could use her things for your nativity scene."

"Thanks, Jack." Jayne fingered the bright-colored beads. "These will be great for the three kings to wear. And I can just imagine these golden slippers on some lucky angel's feet. I'll make sure they get back to you."

Jack waved his hand. "Don't worry. It's about time I started getting rid of a few things. I know Harris would appreciate it if I didn't leave all these messes behind when I go."

Jayne reached over and touched Jack's arm. "I wish you wouldn't talk like that, Jack. I don't want you going anywhere."

"Aw, I'm just a useless old man," said Jack. "Good for nothing."

"Don't say that, Jack. Harris needs you. More than you probably know. And believe it or not, I need you, too."

Jack smiled. "Really? I always think you young people would be glad to get rid of us old codgers. Then you could run this world yourself."

Jayne frowned. "I can't even imagine what a bleak place this world would be if there were no old folks around. You guys are supposed to have all the wisdom, you know. We need you to stick around." Jayne looked up at the clock. "I told Katherine I'd meet her at the crafter's mall before closing today, so I guess I'd better go, Jack. Thanks again for these things. The kids will love them."

Jayne waited for Katherine at their booth. She had two new quilted pillows and several pot holders to add to their inventory but was surprised to see how bare and picked over the booth looked. From the way things were going, their stock wouldn't last through the rest of the Christmas shopping season. The extra money had proved helpful for Jayne, but she couldn't make things fast enough to keep the booth stocked, and Katherine and Joanne's pottery seemed to fly off the shelves.

She knew that Katherine was bringing some new pottery today, as well as some weaving. But at this rate, the booth would probably be empty by next weekend.

Suddenly she had an idea. Maybe the Bible Club kids could make things to sell. Some of them had proved to be very gifted during the craft sessions. If they earned enough money, they could use it toward doing something big, like taking a trip somewhere. When Jayne was a child, an aunt had sent her to a Christian youth camp for a week, and that had been a life-changing experience for her. She would love to see these children have that opportunity.

"Hi there," said Katherine as she set down a cardboard box. "Goodness, there's hardly anything here. I'm glad we're restocking it today."

"Yes, I was just thinking that it will probably be empty again by next weekend, which has given me an idea."

"And what would that be?" Katherine began to unwrap layers of newspaper from a pot. Jayne picked up another one to help.

"Well, I got to thinking how good the Bible Club kids are at making craft items, and how much they enjoy doing it. What if they made things—maybe Christmas things to start out with—to sell here?"

Katherine nodded. "They would probably enjoy doing that, but what would the purpose be, other than helping us to keep the booth stocked?"

"Well, you know how kids enjoy working toward something. I was wondering if there might be a summer camp or something—"

"Jayne, that's a great idea. I bet Pastor Conroy would know of something like that. It would be so fun to take the kids to a camp. They have so much time on their hands in the summer, and this way, we could keep the club going. And it wouldn't matter if we didn't have much time during Christmas to make things—what with the nativity plans—because we could have them make things year 'round."

Jayne smiled. "We'll have to tell the kids on Saturday."

"Great. Did you ask Harris about having a Christmas tree in the barn?"

Jayne nodded. "As usual, he wasn't too excited about it. That man!" She rolled her eyes.

"Yes?" Katherine gestured for her to continue.

"Well, it's been another quiet week. I didn't actually have another conversation with him until yesterday when I mentioned the tree. And he said it was okay, but he seemed kind of grumpy about it—almost as if he was having second thoughts about having Bible Club in his barn. Sometimes I just can't figure him out, Katherine. It's one step forward and two steps back. Just when I think we're really connecting, the next day he acts like we've never met before. It is so frustrating!"

Katherine laughed. "Remember, you're supposed to be a patient yo-yo."

Jayne groaned. "I don't know if I can keep it up. Someday this yo-yo might just accidentally bounce a little too high and pop him one in the nose."

Katherine set the last pot on the shelf. "Might do him some good."

The church donated a nice, tall fir tree for the Bible Club. Pastor Conroy brought over several strings of lights, and an old lady in the congregation loaned them a box full of old Christmas tree ornaments that had been sitting in her attic. Jayne supervised the decorating as children arrived. Later

Katherine would explain the origins of some of the traditional Christmas decorations and how they actually were symbols of more meaningful things. But first they would make plans for the living nativity.

"I have an announcement," said Katherine over the noise of the children. "Listen, everyone! Pastor Conroy just told me today that everything's settled. The living nativity will be held in the city park."

The kids clapped and cheered, and soon everyone was talking at once again, telling about what they had brought for a costume and what animals they could bring and what part they wanted to play. Finally Jayne got everyone seated on the hay bales and pulled out a clipboard.

"Okay. I've made a list of the characters we'll need for the nativity. Of course, there can only be one Mary and Joseph, but there can be lots of angels and shepherds, and the Bible never says exactly how many wise men came...." She looked at the children. "So who wants to be an angel?"

Before long she had several angels and shepherds, but almost every girl wanted to be Mary. The boys were a little more shy, but she could tell that there were several who were hoping to be Joseph.

"I think we should vote for who will be Mary and Joseph," said Katherine. "And so no one's feelings get hurt, let's write it on slips of paper." Autumn handed out pink slips for Mary and blue slips for Joseph. "Now," said Katherine, "we need for you to stand up if you wish to be voted upon. Girls for Mary, and boys for Joseph."

A number of girls stood, including Autumn and Rose. A couple of boys stood; then at the last moment, Sam, the one who was in charge of building, stood too. The barn grew quiet as the children wrote down their votes. Jayne and Katherine quickly collected and counted them while the children had refreshments.

Before Katherine began storytime, she announced how the voting turned out. "It was a tight race, but Rose was chosen to be Mary." Jayne was standing next to Autumn and gave her a little smile, hoping that Autumn wouldn't take it too hard. But she noticed Autumn's lower lip quiver. Katherine continued, "And Sam will be Joseph." Some disappointments were voiced, but for the most part everyone seemed pleased with the choices.

After the rest of the kids were gone, Jayne turned to Autumn. "Autumn, if you want to be an angel, I have this really great pair of golden shoes that Jack donated."

Autumn looked up with sad eyes. "I really wanted to be Mary."

"I know, sweetheart. But you would make a gorgeous angel."

"You think so?"

Jayne nodded. "And I bet the shoes will fit you perfectly. I think they're a size six. Harris's mom must've had small feet."

"That's the same size I wear."

"See, it must have been meant to be."

Autumn's eyes brightened. She pointed to the tree. "Doesn't it look pretty? I thought maybe we could use it at the live nativity, too. That way more people can enjoy it."

Word got around fast that there would be a live nativity in the city park. It was the talk of the town, but not everyone was happy about it. In fact, it seemed that those who talked the most and the loudest were those who were adamantly opposed to the idea. Before the week was over, several editorials had appeared in the local newspaper attacking their plans. One person cited the separation of church and state, and two others complained that Indians should keep their festivities confined to the reservation.

Jayne couldn't believe that anyone would actually have the nerve to write such bigoted things in a public paper. Even worse than that, it felt as if they were attacking the very heart of Christmas. She remembered that Harris had warned her about how this town was set in its ways and change didn't come easily, but she had never expected anything like this. In the teachers' room at school, strong opinions and heated debates could be overheard, and both she and Katherine made every effort to avoid them. But it was comforting to know that there were some people who agreed with them. Jayne decided that this town could be full of surprises. In some ways it reminded her of her relationship with Harris.

On Thursday night, after a long ride on Bailey and a hot soak in the tub, Jayne decided to write her own letter to the editor of the local newspaper. She had been stewing over the possibility all day. She had never done such a thing in her life, and wasn't even sure if she was brave enough to send it in. Maybe she would just write it for herself and then throw it away. She wasn't sure what she would say, but she knew what she wanted the letter to do: to cut past the pettiness, the divisions, and the bigotry, and go straight to the heart of the community.

She prayed for the right words, and then she began to write. When she was finished, she laid the letter on her kitchen table and made herself a cup of tea. She sipped the hot tea, and from across the room she stared at the sheet of paper, wondering if she should just throw it away. But at last she picked it up and read it.

Dear Editor,

I am a newcomer to this town, and I realize there are many things that I don't understand about your life here. And so I have some questions:

1) I see a great deal of patriotism here, and I would expect there to be great respect for our Constitution—but do you believe that "all men are created equal"?

2) I see that children are important to this town, and you call yourselves a "family town," but are you speaking only of white families and white children?

3) I also see lots of churches in this town, along with many decorations to celebrate Christmas, but when a group of children attempts to show Christmas spirit by sharing a live nativity scene in a public park, why is there so much protest?

As I said, I am a newcomer. Perhaps I don't understand, but I like this town and would like to stay here for some time. Can anyone answer my questions?

Sincerely,

Jayne Morgan

Jayne folded the letter and put it in an envelope, still unsure whether or not she would send it. She addressed it and put it in her purse. At least she felt better. She would think about what to do with the letter tomorrow.

EIGHTEEN

◆

J ayne avoided the office area and teachers' room all week, only slipping in to check her mailbox on her way out the door each day. She was tired of hearing about the controversy and tired of being asked ridiculous questions. She hoped that everyone else would soon grow weary of it too. At least today was Friday, and she would have a little break during the weekend. But she was also concerned for the kids at Bible Club. She hoped that all these thoughtless adults wouldn't put a damper on the kids' enthusiasm. Katherine mentioned that Black Hawk was launching a campaign against them on the reservation, even getting the council elders involved.

Jayne pulled her mail out of the wooden slot and absently riffled through the small pile. There were a wedding shower invitation for one of the student teachers, an announcement for the faculty Christmas party, a memo about immunizations, and finally a thin envelope from the school district administration.

She waited until she was in her car to open the official-looking envelope. Considering the general atmosphere around town, she had a feeling it wasn't going to be good. It was a short letter, and she scanned the words quickly, wanting to make sure it wasn't something really horrible. And then she started at the beginning, taking time to read more slowly this time.

It was unbelievable. Simply because Steve Howard had sent a written complaint to the school board, the school district was sending her an official warning. They hadn't even bothered to inquire whether his accusations were true or not. They were actually accusing her of using her teaching position as a platform to promote her political agenda and religious beliefs. All she had done was teach history! What was wrong with these people? Where was the justice in this town? Indignant tears burned in her eyes as she drove to her apartment.

What good was it to try to do the right thing when this was the thanks you got for it? A big slap in the face. All she wanted to do was to help bring people together. To reach out to people on the reservation. Was that so wrong? But lately, it seemed that everywhere she turned someone was pointing a finger at her. She longed to spill her troubles to Katherine. She knew Katherine would understand, because she was going through much the same experience. But Katherine had taken Autumn to the orthodontist this afternoon, and then they were going to her mother's for supper. Jayne felt very alone.

Just then she thought of Bailey, and suddenly she felt better. She raced up the stairs to her apartment and quickly pulled on her riding gear. She paused by the mirror to survey the damage of her tearstained face. Hopefully she wouldn't see Harris today. She wasn't too worried since he had been avoiding her all week. And why shouldn't he? She was probably embarrassing him again. It must be hard for him to have such a radical nut spending so much time at his place. She looked at her English riding attire in the mirror. It did look foreign. Nobody dressed like that in this town. She remembered how much it had bothered Harris initially, but slowly she had thought he'd gotten used to it. Perhaps he hadn't; maybe he only tolerated it to be polite. Maybe he only tolerated her out of politeness too. That could explain his on-again, off-again behavior.

The more she thought about it, the more she realized she didn't fit into this strange little cowboy town. First she had been jilted by one of the town's elite. Never mind that he had proved to be a first-rate jerk, which certainly didn't speak well of her judgment. Even her job had been the result of someone knowing the right person, and right now that job seemed to be in serious jeopardy. She rode the wrong kind of horse, and she rode him the wrong way. On top of that, she was much too fond of her horse. What a joke she must be to everyone. It almost made her laugh. Almost.

Instead she called her mother.

"Hello?"

"Hi, Mom," said Jayne, trying to sound cheerful.

"Hello, Jayne. Is everything okay?"

"Sure. I just needed to hear a friendly voice. It's been a rough week."

"That's too bad. It's been a rough week here, too. My allergies are acting up again. Sometimes it feels like I can hardly breathe. I've had the air purifier running night and day. And then I've had these migraine headaches, and—"

"How's Daddy?" Jayne interrupted. It was funny how being away from home had almost made her forget her mother's bouts with hypochondria.

"Oh, your father's just fine, as usual." The way she said it sounded as if being fine were something to be ashamed of. "How are you, Jayne?"

"I'm fine, too. I didn't really have much to say. I just wanted to say hi."

"Well, that was nice of you. I've been meaning to call you, too. Are you coming home for Christmas?"

"I hadn't really given it much thought yet. Right now we're working with this group of kids to set up a live nativity for Christmas, and—"

"Oh, that's nice, dear." This time her mother cut her off.

"But I just don't know how you can stand to be around all those animals and that dusty hay and everything. It would absolutely kill me with my allergies. You know, the doctor has actually suggested that I move to Arizona before I develop asthma."

"Well, I guess it's a good thing that I don't suffer from allergies since I love the smell of hay and animals. And speaking of animals, Mom, I was just on my way out the door. I'm off to ride Bailey now. But it was nice talking with you. Give Dad my love. I'll think about Christmas and let you know."

"Well, give that beast of yours a pat for me, Jayne. And you ride carefully now."

"I always do. Thanks for talking, Mom."

Jayne felt slightly better as she drove out to the ranch. Somehow hearing her mother's complaints made her feel a little stronger. Maybe she was just glad not to be living that sort of life. Or maybe she was thankful that she didn't have the same phobias as her mother.

She was barely out of her car when Bailey came trotting over to her. He gave his dark mane a shake and snorted as if to say hello. She knew that an hour or two on his back would probably set the world straight again. There was nothing like horse therapy. If scientists could think of a way to bottle the stuff, they could make millions.

Little puffs of frosty air came out of his nostrils. It was getting colder each day, and it had been freezing at night. She wondered if they might get some snow before long. It had been ages since she had seen a white Christmas, but maybe this year would be different. She took in a deep breath. Yes, she was definitely feeling better already. For a couple of hours, she would put her troubles out of her mind. After all, she had all weekend to worry about them. Not that worrying would help.

She saddled up Bailey and had one foot in the stirrup when she heard Harris's voice. It figured. All week long she had been hoping to chat with him, and now, just when she didn't want to see him, he showed up.

"Hi, Jayne. You taking off on a ride?"

She turned and looked over her shoulder. He was striding purposefully toward her, and she realized it would be impossible to ride off without a few words. She removed her foot from the stirrup and turned to face him.

"I was just about to. The fact is, I really need a ride before I go totally bonkers. It's been one of those weeks." She hoped her voice conveyed that she was in no mood for chitchat.

Harris nodded. "Yeah, from what I hear, things are getting pretty heated up about your Bible Club and that nativity thing in the park."

Jayne rolled her eyes and sighed. "Yes, and I find it incredibly hard to believe how narrow-minded some people can be."

"Well, Jayne," he said in his cowboy drawl, "it's like I said, you need to take things slow and easy around here." Jayne's eyes narrowed as she prepared herself for what sounded like some sort of lecture. "You see, these folks are used to doing things a certain way. They've been doing it this way for years. You've got to understand that change just doesn't come that easy for them—"

"Does change come at all?" she snapped, unable to hold herself back. "Sometimes I think I've gone back in time. Sometimes it feels like you people live in the nineteenth century around here—like the Old West cowboys and Indians! Doesn't this town know that times have changed? Do you think these people realize they're about to enter the twenty-first century and they totally missed the twentieth?"

"See, there you go, Jayne. Charging with both barrels

loaded." He chuckled. "Maybe we should start calling you Calamity Jayne."

Jayne pressed her lips together and glared at him, but Harris didn't seem to notice. She turned and got ready to mount her horse, as mad at herself for losing her temper as she was mad at him for pushing her.

"Now, don't you go off all mad, Calamity. I didn't mean to hurt your feelings. I'm just trying to—"

"Do you even care about my feelings?" She turned and faced him. "Or are you just like the rest of this town?" He looked surprised, maybe even ashamed, but he said nothing, and so she continued. She might as well get it all out. "That's right, isn't it, Harris? You've been judging me ever since I came here. I've got the wrong kind of horse. I hang out with the wrong kind of people. I probably went to the wrong kind of school. I almost married the wrong guy." She looked down at her clothes. "And I wear the wrong kind of clothes—"

"Well, maybe if you tried to fit in a little bit more, instead of being so stuck in your highfalutin ways. Yeah, we do live differently here. But we like it! And if you want to live here happily and peacefully, you might need to make some adjustments. Maybe even a few compromises. Do you think it's fair for you to come in here and expect all of us to do the changing while you just go merrily along?"

"Fine!" She ripped open her chin strap and threw her riding helmet and crop on the ground, then pulled off her long tweed riding jacket and tossed it on the fence. "There, is that better? I'm sure I've embarrassed you by riding English on your property. Next time I come out, I'll be sure to wear my cowboy boots and Wranglers, and maybe I can find a big ol' rodeo belt. Would that make you happy?"

She turned and in one swing was in the saddle. She dug her

knees sharply into Bailey's sides, and he took off in a flash. Then she squeezed him again, urging him into a full run. She could no longer see because of the tears in her eyes, so she gave him the lead, knowing she could trust him. The wind was as sharp as ice, and without her jacket she quickly grew numb, but she didn't care. All she wanted was to get away. Away from Harris. Away from a town that didn't care. Away from judgmental school boards. And perhaps most of all, she wanted to get away from herself. She didn't like the way she had just acted. And as much as she wanted to blame Harris and everyone else, she knew that when the day was done, it was her own face she would have to look at in the mirror.

When she could finally see where they were going, she realized that Bailey had run all the way across the recently harvested stubble field and was now heading straight into the winter wheat field. Harris had already told her in no uncertain terms that this was out of bounds for riding. The green grass blades were only a few inches tall, and Bailey's hooves would tear up the tender shoots, so she leaned sharply to the left and firmly pulled him away from the planted field.

In the same instant, an explosion of feathers and wings and squawking filled the air as a frightened pheasant rooster shot straight up from the stubble. The next thing she knew, Bailey was rearing to the right, but she continued to move to the left. She flew out of the saddle. As she was falling, she could see Bailey's front legs crumble beneath him. And then the world turned completely black.

NINETEEN

◆

Jayne raced on bare feet through the wheat field, trying to catch something, or someone. What was it she was chasing? Suddenly she remembered—Bailey! Where had he vanished to? She looked and looked, but everything was hazy and dim. Unreal. Bailey was nowhere to be seen. She called and called his name, but he did not come to her. She whistled, but he did not respond. Where could he have gone?

She walked on and on until her feet bled, but she could not feel them. They didn't hurt at all. The sky grew dark and low. And still she could not find Bailey. Then she heard a high-pitched wailing sound, almost like a fire siren or someone crying. Maybe it was Bailey. Was he hurt? Was he crying for her? She had to find him, she had to save him! She thought she heard Harris calling her name, asking if she could hear him. But she couldn't see Harris anywhere. Was he angry that she had trampled his wheat? She heard his voice again, but he didn't sound angry. He sounded sad.

"Harris!" she cried out, but she couldn't hear her own voice. She cried out again. "Find Bailey! Help him, Harris, he's hurt!" And then no more words would come out of her. She tried and tried, but there was nothing. Only thick blackness again, covering her like a blanket of quicksand. Burying her. And she was cold. Very cold.

Later—and she knew it was later, but she didn't know when it was or where—Katherine came riding by on her horse. Riding bareback. At first Katherine was waving, as if she were in a parade. But she was galloping fast. Her feet were bare, and she wore a beautiful white leather dress. Long strands of white fringe flapped gently in the breeze as she rode, and her long, dark hair floated loosely behind her. But as she drew closer, Jayne saw the look of terror in her eyes.

"Run for your life, Jayne!" she screamed. But already her voice was far away, almost an echo in the distance. When Jayne looked back from where Katherine had come, she saw a group of cowboys riding fast and hard. They looked like a posse, and they had their rifles raised and aimed. They approached in a cloud of dust, with the thundering of dozens of hooves. Jayne crouched low in the wheat field, hoping desperately that they would not see her. Oh, if only she could find Bailey. She would hop on his back and ride away.

At last she saw Bailey. But he was running away from her. Running fast. He would not come when she called his name. He would not even turn his head and look at her. She cried and cried for him, but he would not come. Then she saw the yellow tractor coming, with the big low trailer behind it. It was moving slowly, but it was following Bailey. It was the trailer they put dead animals on. She told the tractor to stop, but it kept going. It kept following Bailey. She sobbed and sobbed. She begged the tractor to stay away from her horse. But it kept going until she could no longer see it.

She was so tired. She just wanted to sleep. But she thought she heard Harris calling to her. Then he was speaking. His voice sounded calm and peaceful. His voice was like a rope, and she wanted to hang on to it, but she couldn't understand the words he said. She thought she heard him praying.

And then she was praying, too. The words were only in her head, but she knew that God could hear her. And she thought she could hear his voice, but he didn't speak in words. It was more like music and warmth and light, all mixed together in a beautiful, sunny symphony that she wanted never to end.

TWENTY

◆

"J ayne?" She could hear Harris's voice, but it sounded as if he were in a long, padded tunnel. "Jayne? Can you hear me? Just squeeze my fingers if you can hear me."

She tried to speak, but no words came out. She told her fingers to obey her mind and to tighten, but she wasn't sure if her fingers were connected to her thoughts.

"I felt that, Jayne!" His voice sounded a little closer now. "Come back to us, Jayne," he pleaded. "Please, come back."

She thought of the warmth and sunlight of the world behind her, but then she felt Harris's hand upon hers. And it was warm. It almost seemed as if she had to make a decision. Did she want to stay here with Harris, or return to—where?

"Jayne, I know you can hear me," he said. Now his voice sounded as if it was in the same room. "I'm so sorry I said those things. Won't you please come back to us? Come back to me, Jayne."

She willed her hand to squeeze his fingers. She wanted to speak. She wanted to come back. She knew she was ready to come back. But she wasn't sure if it was within her power to do so. She asked God to allow her to come back. Then she relaxed and waited. And waited.

When she finally opened her eyes, Harris was not there. She wondered if he had actually been there at all. She saw a fluorescent light above her bed. She could see that she was in a hospital room, although she did not recall coming here. The last thing she could remember was falling. What had happened

223

to Bailey? Was he even alive? Maybe she didn't want to know the answer yet. She tried to look around, but it hurt to move her head. She wondered what time it was. How long had she been here? Was it still Friday, or was it the next day?

The room had Christmas decorations hanging here and there. A strand of green tinsel was draped in swags from the ceiling just above the foot of her bed. Brightly colored tree ornaments were suspended from it. They looked homemade, as if by children. There were lots of cards and flower arrangements on a nearby table, and even some stuffed animals, including a reindeer with a bell around his neck and a black-and-white spotted pony. There were several poinsettia plants on a table by the door. Everything looked strange to her. Maybe they had put her in someone else's room, someone who had checked out and forgotten to take all these things home with them.

"Miss Morgan!" A short blond woman in a nurse's uniform came into the room. "At last you're awake!" She smiled at Jayne and immediately began checking her, looking into her eyes, checking her pulse, her blood pressure. "I'll be right back. I want to notify the doctor." The nurse squeezed her hand. "Now don't you go away."

Jayne wondered where she would try to go. She opened her mouth to speak, but her throat felt bone-dry, and all that came out was a gasp.

"We'll get you something to drink," said the nurse as she hurried out the door. Jayne carefully turned her head and looked out the open door but could only see the door to a room on the other side of the hall. She closed her eyes and tried to relax, but it was strange being stuck in a bed with an IV hooked to her.

"Jayne!" cried a familiar voice that could only belong to her mother. "Oh, Jayne, you're okay! I've been so worried about you."

Jayne looked up to see her mother hovering over her, peering down through thick-lensed glasses. She was holding a paper cup with a straw. "Here, Jayne, the nurse said you could have a sip of water. Not too much now. Just a tiny sip." Her mother held the straw to her cracked lips and Jayne sipped gratefully. Then her mother moved the cup away.

"Is it still Friday?" The words were audible, but hoarse. Jayne looked at her mother's troubled face and waited.

"No, dear. Let's see, I guess it's Wednesday now. I flew from Portland on Saturday morning. Your father got here Sunday night. You've been unconscious for days, Jayne. It's been perfectly horrible. Everyone has been so worried. And the doctor wasn't sure if you'd ever wake up." Tears trickled down her mother's smooth cheeks, and suddenly she looked much older than Jayne remembered. She took off her glasses and wiped her eyes with a pale pink handkerchief, then blew her nose.

"It's okay, Mom," whispered Jayne. "I'm all right."

"Everyone will be so relieved, Jayne. Your father is getting something to eat in the cafeteria. I think his ulcer is starting to act up again. I told him to get some soup."

Jayne nodded. "That's good."

"And we've met so many of your friends, Jayne. Why, I had no idea that you had so many friends, dear. After only being here for such a short while."

"Who do you mean?"

"Oh, just about everyone, I'm sure. In fact, your friend Harris is with your father right now. He seems like a very nice young man. His father is nice too. And Katherine will probably be here in a few hours. She always comes in around noon, after she finishes teaching. I think she said today was the last day before Christmas vacation."

Her mother pointed to the decorations. "Katherine brought these for you. The students in your class made them. It sounds as if they've really missed you, Jayne. I think there are some other things from them on the table there. And it's rather strange, but a lot of Indian children have dropped by. There are a lot of cards over there. Katherine says they're from your Bible Club. You do seem to have plenty of friends, Jayne. And they all seem very nice."

Jayne smiled and closed her eyes, suddenly very tired. "Yes, they are."

"Just rest a little, Jayne. The doctor should be here any minute."

The next time Jayne opened her eyes, she saw a strange gray-haired man standing above her. He peered down at her, checking her ears and eyes and pulse. He even asked her some questions about what year it was and who was president. Then he stuck his stethoscope into his pocket. "Well, little lady, it looks like you're on the road to recovery. I had them run a CAT scan while you were unconscious. Other than a slight swelling that is normal for a head injury of that nature, everything looked fine."

"Why was I unconscious for so long?" asked Jayne.

"Head injuries are a mysterious thing, Jayne. But the body's way of dealing with them is to go into a deep sleep, which as it turns out is the best medicine. You see, the brain needs to remain immobile to heal. Of course, we don't want anyone to stay in a coma for too long. We get a little uneasy when it lasts longer than a day or two. But everything seems normal. We'll observe you for the remainder of the day. Barring any unforeseen complications, you ought to be able to go home tomorrow, if you have someone who can care for you. You'll still need a few days of rest to recover."

The doctor finally stepped away, and Jayne noticed Harris in the hallway, standing next to her dad. Harris stared with wide, hopeful eyes, a cautious smile playing across his lips. He lifted his hand slightly, as if to wave.

"Harris?" she called. He was instantly by her side.

"Jayné, I'm so thankful you're finally awake. It's been so long. It seems like weeks. How are you feeling?"

"Okay, I guess, under the circumstances."

"I'm so sorry, Jayne. If only you'd had your riding helmet on." He looked down at his hands. "I feel like this whole thing is all my fault—"

"Don't, Harris. I'm not a child. I did what I did of my own free will. And it was incredibly foolish." Suddenly her eyes began to fill with tears as she remembered how Bailey had fallen. "Harris." She choked the words out. "Is Bailey all right?"

Harris took her hand in his and nodded. "He's fine, Jayne. I've had the vet out twice just to make sure. I've been looking after him myself. He has a bad sprain on his right forefoot, but that's all. I've been keeping it wrapped and he's staying in a box stall." Harris looked over his shoulder as he spoke in a hushed, confidential tone. "And don't tell anyone this, but I've been babying him, Jayne. I'm trying to take care of him the way I thought you would."

Jayne smiled. "Thanks, Harris."

"You actually mumbled something about helping Bailey while the ambulance was coming."

"I had such strange dreams," said Jayne. She wanted to tell Harris all about it, but then she remembered her dad. He was standing patiently at the end of the bed with his hands in his pockets. She realized that she hadn't even spoken to him yet. "Hi, Daddy," she said, smiling weakly. "How are you doing?"

He stepped closer, and she could see the traces of tears in his eyes. "We've been worried sick about you, Jayne." This surprised her since her dad had never been one to show much emotion.

"I'm okay, Daddy."

He bent over and hugged her, holding her tight for a long moment. "I'm so glad, Jayne," he sobbed. "So glad."

Her parents stayed and quietly visited for a while, but soon the nurse came back and told them that they should let Jayne get some more rest.

"Now that you're okay," her dad said apologetically, "I should probably head back home. I hate to go, but there's work, and I left everything in such a hurry—"

"It's okay, Daddy," said Jayne. "I'll be fine. You go ahead and go. If you leave soon, you won't even have to drive after dark. I know how you hate driving at night."

He looked at his watch. "The doctor says you'll be just fine. And I don't expect there's much I can do...."

Jayne looked at her mother. "You should probably go home with Dad, too," she said gently.

"I can't just leave you here—"

"But Mom, you hate to fly. And don't worry, I'll be fine. The doctor said I could go home tomorrow."

"And your friend Katherine did say that you could stay at her house to recover." Her mom looked over to her dad, searching for reassurance.

"Really," said Jayne, "I'll be okay. I appreciate you both coming. But I understand that you need to get back." Part of Jayne wanted her parents to stay, but the rational side of her knew that it could end up being more trouble than help. If they stayed, she would probably feel responsible for them. Her apartment was so tiny and not set up for visitors. In the long run, she knew it would probably be easier for everyone if they just went back home.

"Okay, honey," said her mom as she picked up her purse. "Katherine has your clothes and purse and whatnot. I noticed you had a letter all ready to send, so I went ahead and mailed it for you."

Jayne tried to recall what letter it could be. "You mean *in* my purse?"

"Yes. I think it was for your newspaper subscription or something. I put a stamp on it and sent it."

Jayne swallowed hard. It was her letter to the editor. "When did you mail it?" she asked weakly.

"On Saturday. Now, you're sure you'll be fine without us?" She patted Jayne on the arm.

"Positive," said Jayne as she forced a smile to her lips. Why had her mother mailed that letter? Better yet, why had she ever written it?

Good-byes were said, and her parents finally left. Jayne closed her eyes and tried to rest, but all she could think of was that stupid letter. But perhaps it wasn't too late. Perhaps the paper hadn't run it yet. She could call them up and tell them it was a big mistake and ask them to throw it away. But before she could do anything she drifted off to sleep.

When she awoke, Harris was sitting by her side.

He smiled down on her. "How are you feeling?" he asked quietly.

She stared up at him. It was odd seeing Harris in this sterile setting. She was so used to seeing him outside working in the fields, with dirt on his hands and the blue sky behind him. He looked strangely out of place here in the hospital. But then she probably did too 'In fact, she probably looked awful. She reached her hand up to her head to feel the place where it still ached.

"You've got a bit of a lump," said Harris with a slight frown.

"I must look horrible."

Harris smiled. "Well, I've seen you looking better."

She wanted to ask him for a mirror, but then thought it might be just as well not to know. "Have you read the paper lately?" she asked.

His face looked puzzled. "You mean the newspaper?"

"Yes. Have you been reading it?"

"Well, I've glanced at it from time to time. But I guess I haven't been paying real close attention. Why?"

"You haven't read the editorial page?"

"Not that I recall. Why?"

Jayne sighed. "Oh, I wrote this silly letter. Just a response to all the letters that were attacking the living nativity in the park. But I never meant to send it."

Harris was clearly confused.

"My mother found it in my purse, and it seems she mailed it for me on Saturday."

Harris nodded. "I see. And now you're feeling concerned."

"I never would have sent it."

"Well, maybe it will all turn out for the best."

Jayne studied his face. Suddenly he looked serious. Too serious. "Maybe so," she muttered, then closed her eyes.

"Do you need to rest again?" he asked quietly.

She opened her eyes and looked at him. His eyes were so blue. They would always remind her of the sky. "No. I don't think so," she said, keeping her eyes fixed on his.

"Will it wear you out if I talk to you a little?"

"No, that would be nice."

"Well, while you were unconscious, I did a lot of thinking. Maybe it was soul-searching, I don't know. But anyway, I asked myself some pretty tough questions. I know that Dad told you about how Jill Emerson died, and I expect he told you that I took it real hard. And then, of course, on top of that I had already seen my mom die. And then Paul lost his wife to cancer.... Well, I guess I just figured it might be better to be alone than to love someone and lose them again. It seemed to me that it's just the way things go. And it wasn't such a bad way to live. Playing it safe, and all." Harris looked up at the ceiling. She saw him swallow and then sigh deeply. This wasn't easy for him.

"I can understand that, Harris," she said.

"It was real hard watching you in this hospital bed, day after day, not knowing if you were ever going to wake up. And feeling like it was my fault that you were even—"

"Harris, I told you—it was my fault."

He shook his head. "No, if I hadn't said—"

"Let it go, Harris. It's over and done now. I'm going to be fine. And believe me, next time I ride, and there's definitely going to be a next time, I *will* be wearing my riding helmet."

"Good. And, Jayne, I promise I'll never give you a bad time about all your funny English riding gear again. But what I wanted to say—"

"Hey, there!" called Katherine as she burst into the room. "You're awake at last, Jayne! The nurse just told me that you're going to be fine." In the next instant, Katherine had her arms around Jayne.

"It's so good to see you, Katherine," said Jayne when Katherine finally pulled away. Jayne was touched to see tears on Katherine's cheeks.

"Not nearly as good as it is to see you. Although you do

231

look a sight. Have you seen yourself?"

"No, but I've been wondering. Is there a mirror around?"

Katherine dug a hand mirror out of the drawer. "Are you sure you want to look?"

Jayne reached for the mirror. It was pretty bad. She had a large bruise on her forehead that was several shades of green and brown. Under her eyes were the purple remnants of what must have been very black eyes. Beneath the bruises, her skin was a pasty white. She handed the mirror back to Katherine and groaned. "Sorry I asked."

"I guess I should have left the mirror hidden," said Katherine. "But believe it or not, you actually look a lot better than you did a couple days back." She squeezed her hand. "I'm so glad you're really okay." Katherine looked at Harris, then back at Jayne. "Did you guys see yesterday's paper?"

"The editorial page?" asked Jayne, not really wanting to hear the answer.

"Way to go, Jayne!" said Katherine. She held up her thumb. "That was really great."

Jayne groaned. "I can't believe they printed it. I'll probably be run out of town now. Or maybe they'll just slip something into my IV."

Katherine laughed. "Well, I suppose we could get a guard posted. But I think most of the people in town are applauding you."

"Really?" Jayne looked up to see if Katherine was kidding.

"Yes, you should have heard them at school today. Everyone thought it was great. Even the ones who were arguing against you last week were singing a different tune today. It was really amazing. The timing on that letter couldn't have been better. How in the world did you pull it off? Did you send it before the accident?"

"No, I wasn't going to send it at all. My mom found it and sent it. Were the teachers really supportive?"

Katherine nodded. "Yes. Greg Williams even said that he was going to write another letter to back yours up."

"I can't believe it." She looked at Harris. "I guess you were right."

He shook his head as if he didn't remember.

"You said it might work out for the best."

"Well, you know what they say," he remarked with a grin. "God works in mysterious ways." He glanced at his watch. "Well, you seem to be in good hands, Jayne. And you'll probably appreciate it if I get back before dark to check on Bailey and feed the critters."

"Yes. And tell Bailey that I'm fine and will be back in the saddle again before long."

Harris winked. "Just don't make me kiss him for you."

"Not this time," said Jayne.

Shortly after Harris left, Pastor Conroy stopped in for a while, then a couple of teachers dropped by with cards. Everyone was pleased to see that Jayne was better. And Jayne was pleased to see that they cared. Katherine gathered all the cards and things that had been dropped off and brought them over to the bed.

As Jayne glanced through them, she was surprised to find one from Black Hawk. She held up the card to Katherine. It had a picture of a wolf on it. "I can't believe Black Hawk actually sent me a card."

Katherine smiled. "He comes across as a brute, but he really does have a heart."

There was a card from the Long family, sent by Derrick's mother. The spotted stuffed pony was from Harris. It had a card attached that read, "I know this doesn't look much like

Bailey, but I thought you might enjoy it. Love, Harris." Jayne blushed as she slipped the card back into the envelope. She wondered what it was that Harris had been about to tell her. But she was afraid to get her hopes up. After all, she knew how Harris could go back and forth.

The next morning, Katherine and Autumn helped Jayne check out of the hospital and then took her home. They had a room all ready for her, but Jayne didn't want to sleep anymore.

"Please, don't make me go to bed," she begged like a small child. "I've been in bed for days. Can't I just—"

"Jayne, I promised the doctor that you'd rest in bed for most of the day," said Katherine. "So just try and help out here, okay? At least lie down for an hour or so. Then maybe if you're good, you can get up."

"I want to see Bailey," pleaded Jayne.

"Not today," said Katherine with school-teacher authority.

The day passed slowly, but by evening, Jayne had convinced Katherine that she was well enough to be up. But she still couldn't talk her into letting her go check on Bailey. After dinner, Jayne hoped that perhaps Harris would stop by for a visit. But he did not.

She went to bed that night wondering if she had imagined that Harris was trying to tell her something in the hospital the day before. Why had she allowed herself to get her hopes up?

The next morning, Jayne woke early. She was still a little weak, but her head didn't hurt anymore, and she was pretty sure she could make the walk over to Harris's to see Bailey. She made a pot of coffee, then sat down and looked longingly out across the field that ran between Katherine's house and Harris's property. It did look kind of far.

"Planning your escape?" asked Katherine. She walked into

the kitchen and poured herself a cup of coffee, then sat down across from Jayne.

"How'd you guess?"

"I know that you're dying to see that old horse of yours. How about if I drive you over this afternoon? I have to take Autumn to a party this morning. And then I promised Mom I would stop by if you were feeling okay. Are you okay?"

"Sure, I'm fine. Whose party?"

"Rose's. She's having a birthday party at the skating rink, and she invited Autumn."

"That's great. Say, how are the plans coming for the live nativity? Is it going to work out in the park? Are the kids still doing it?"

Katherine smiled mysteriously. "I guess you'll just have to wait and see. Can you hold out on seeing Bailey until this afternoon?"

"I suppose. Why the mystery?"

"Well, we're still taking care of some details, but hopefully it'll all work out. The kids sure haven't given up yet."

Soon Katherine and Autumn were gone, and Jayne was alone in the house. She sat down and tried to read a magazine, but she felt too restless to focus, and finally she tossed the magazine aside. She looked out the window. The sky was a dull gray and looked so low she thought she could reach up and touch it. Maybe they would have a white Christmas after all. She leaned back on the couch and, closing her eyes, thanked God for bringing her through her recent ordeal as she had so many times in the past few days. The nurse had told her that they had been pretty concerned, and her recovery had seemed almost like a miracle. Jayne thought it was.

"Hello?" called a voice from the porch.

It sounded like Harris. She walked over to the door and opened it to see Harris standing before her with a big grin.

"I thought you might want to get out and see your horse today. That is, if you're feeling all right." Harris glanced around the room as if looking for Katherine. "Is it okay for you to go out?"

"Sure. I would love to see Bailey. Katherine and Autumn are gone. Just let me write a note and get my jacket and shoes." Jayne hurriedly wrote the message and found a jacket of Katherine's to wear. But when she bent over to try to pull on her boots, she grew dizzy. The next thing she knew, Harris was helping to hold her up.

"Are you sure you're okay?" he asked, his eyes wide and full of fear.

She looked into his eyes and remembered the day she had gone out to chastise him about his animals running out of water. He had thought something had happened to Jack, and his eyes had looked just the way they did now.

"Harris, I'm fine," she reassured him. "I'm sure it's perfectly normal to feel dizzy after a head injury."

"Why don't you sit down to put your boots on," he said as he guided her to the couch and then knelt to help her with her boots.

"Thanks." She looked down at him kneeling before her and unexpectedly felt tears in her eyes. It was silly to get choked up over such a small thing. She turned away and blinked.

"Okay," said Harris as he stood and extended his arm. "Let me help you to your carriage, my lady."

She took his arm. "Thank you." It felt good to hold on to him. The rough wool of his jacket felt strong and sturdy. He smelled like hay. She took a deep breath and sighed. He opened the pickup door for her, then turned to help her in. As he did their eyes met once more, and she felt her heart give that odd little twist that was part pain and part pure joy.

"Jayne," he said, then stopped.

"Yes?"

"Have I ever told you that I think you're absolutely beautiful?"

She smiled. "Thanks." He helped her to step up into the pickup, then closed the door behind her. She watched as he walked around to his door, studying his every move, every step. He grinned at her as he started the engine.

"Bailey will be glad to see you."

She nodded, but suddenly seeing Bailey seemed secondary.

"What were you going to say the other day in the hospital, before Katherine got there?" she asked quietly.

Harris glanced at her, then back at the road. Already he was turning into his driveway. "In the hospital?" he said vaguely, as if he didn't recall.

"Yes, you were talking about the losses you've had, and how you had been doing some soul-searching.... Don't you remember? Which one of us had the knock on the head?"

Harris chuckled as he pulled up to the barn. "I guess I remember that conversation. But don't you want to go and see Bailey now?"

"No. I want to talk to you," she answered stubbornly.

"Well, if this doesn't beat all." Harris grinned at her. "You'd rather talk to me than your horse." But he was already climbing out of the pickup and going around to open her door.

She stared at him as he helped her out. "Aren't you going to answer?"

"Maybe. But first I think you need to see Bailey."

She stopped and folded her arms against her chest. "I'm not moving an inch until you answer me."

Harris laughed. "I can't even remember what the question was!"

"What were you going to tell me at the hospital?"

"Oh, you mean that I love you."

She grabbed him by the sleeve and stared into his face, not sure if she had heard him right. "What did you say? I've had a recent head injury, and I may not be understanding you."

He pulled her close to him and said the words slowly and carefully. "I love you, Jayne Morgan. I tried real hard not to. But it was useless. I knew it for sure that day you marched out into my wheat field wearing your silly little riding outfit and then proceeded to yell at me."

She felt as if she were melting in his arms. "You love me?" she repeated stupidly.

"Yes. You pried it out of me, Jayne. Now how about you?"

"Me?" she said dreamily.

"Yes, *you*."

"Well, I love you too." She leaned forward, ready to receive the long-awaited kiss. Ready to be cradled in his arms. Ready to—

"Okay, then. Let's go see your horse."

"What?"

"Bailey. Remember him?"

She nodded incredulously. She stared at Harris as if he had completely lost his marbles. But he didn't seem to notice. He took her by the arm and gently but firmly led her to the horse stalls.

"Here he is," said Harris as he opened the stall door. Jayne just looked at Harris and wondered how she could possibly love such a strange and unpredictable person. But it was too late. She did.

Bailey nickered softly when he saw Jayne. She took one

more curious look at Harris then moved toward Bailey. "Hi there, sweet thing," she said softly as she stroked his velvety nose. "I've missed you. I'm so glad you're getting better." She looked down at his wrapped leg. He was putting pressure on it—a good sign. She rubbed her cheek against his and breathed deeply. He still smelled like a horse. "Don't worry, old boy," she whispered, "I still love you too."

Just then a metallic glint caught her eye. She looked up to see something shiny tied with a piece of red yarn to Bailey's halter. She reached up and untied the string. It was a gold ring, with a good-sized diamond. She turned and looked at Harris. "What's this?" she asked with a catch in her voice.

"Looks like a ring to me."

"I know that. It looks like an engagement ring." She glanced at Bailey. "So does this mean that Bailey wants to marry me?"

Harris laughed. "No. Bailey was just the messenger. I figured that my chances might improve if Bailey helped me out a little."

Now Jayne was laughing. She moved closer to Harris and looked up into his eyes. "So what exactly does this mean, Harris McAllister?"

"It means I'm asking you to marry me. Will you be my wife, Jayne Morgan?" His eyes were fixed on hers, and she felt she was looking into his soul. She knew that she had always loved him. Would always love him.

Jayne swallowed hard, blinking back tears. She threw herself into his arms and blurted, "Of course I'll marry you!"

They stood there for a long time, clinging tightly to each other. Jayne was afraid to let go. Afraid that this was just another of the dreams she had experienced with her head injury. She didn't want it to end, ever.

Then Harris gently took her chin in his hand and tilted it

toward him. And then he kissed her as she had never been kissed before. After a long moment they pulled away and stared into each other's eyes. Jayne could hear Bailey behind her and could smell the sweet hay. Outside the barn, delicate snowflakes were falling down. And she knew it wasn't a dream. It was too good to be a dream.

Later that evening, after Harris had taken Jayne out for dinner, he drove through town. Snow was already blanketing the shops and streets like an old-fashioned Christmas card. Jayne noticed an unusual amount of traffic as they approached the city park.

"What's going on?" she asked as Harris parked the truck.

He took her gently by the arm. "I don't want to wear you out, Jayne, but there's something you have to see."

Many other people had parked their vehicles and were now walking through the snowy park. Ahead of them was a small wooden structure, with animals all about and children dressed like angels and kings and shepherds. And there stood Rose and Sam before a manger. Christmas music was playing over a loudspeaker. Pastor Conroy was on one side, helping to round up a runaway goat.

"You're here!" said Katherine. "Isn't it great?" She proudly pointed to an angel with silver braces and golden slippers. "There's Autumn."

"How did you do it?" asked Jayne.

"By the grace of God," said Katherine. "And a little help from a few friends." She looked at Harris. "Harris helped Sam and the building crew put this structure together. And the city council came through with a special permit to use the park after a certain letter to the editor hit a nerve of many of the townspeople."

Jayne smiled. "It's wonderful." She looked around the crowd to see some familiar faces. Mary Bluefish was standing next to Corky Galloway. A couple of teachers from school were next to them. Katherine's mother was standing on the perimeter with Black Hawk. As usual, Black Hawk had a frown on his face, but at least he had come. Even Harris's friend, Paul Roderick, was there. Everyone seemed to be enjoying the event.

"It feels like a small beginning," said Katherine.

"Yes," sighed Jayne. She reached for Harris's hand. It was strong and warm and enveloped hers like a big leather mitt.

"Thank God for small beginnings," said Harris as he gave her hand a squeeze.

Jayne looked up at Harris and smiled, and he wiped a snowflake from her nose.

Dear Reader,

Some people think that fiction is only "escape reading." But the fact is, we all need an escape from time to time, and what better way than a good book?

I love how fiction can be the vessel that allows us to travel to unexpected places. Occasionally we might face some uncomfortable issues, but somehow, when these issues are wrapped around the lives of characters who are immersed in a plot, it becomes easier for us to look on without feeling pressure to change. My prayer is that the Holy Spirit will use my stories to change lives—according to God's timing.

I think that's one reason Jesus taught with stories. He knew that stories could touch people right where they lived. And even if they didn't have "ears to hear" at that moment, perhaps they would have minds to remember; and later on when they were ready to hear, the story would still be with them.

In *Heartland Skies* I wanted to take a closer look at some of the cultural divisions that exist in our society today. My goal wasn't to set the world straight, but merely to ask the question: is this how God wants us live? I realize that I've barely scratched the surface, but my hope is that this story will remind us that our world is in desperate need of reconciliation. And reconciliation begins in the church—and in each and every one of us.

"Blessed are the peacemakers, for they will be called sons [daughters] of God" (Matthew 5:9).

Melody Carlson

Write to Melody Carlson
c/o Palisades
P.O. Box 1720
Sisters, Oregon 97759

THE PALISADES LINE

Memories, Peggy Darty (May 1998)
ISBN 1-57673-171-5
In this sequel to *Promises*, Elizabeth Calloway is left with amnesia after witnessing a hit-and-run accident. Her husband, Michael, takes her on a vacation to Cancún so that she can relax and recover her memory. What they don't realize is that the killer is following them, hoping to wipe out Elizabeth's memory permanently....

Remembering the Roses, Marion Duckworth (June 1998)
ISBN 1-57673-236-3
Sammie Sternberg is trying to escape her memories of the man who betrayed her, and she ends up in a small town on the Olympic Peninsula in Washington. There she opens her dream business—an antique shop in an old Victorian—and meets a reclusive watercolor artist who helps to heal her broken heart.

Waterfalls, Robin Jones Gunn
ISBN 1-57673-221-5
In a visit to Glenbrooke, Oregon, Meredith Graham meets movie star Jacob Wilde and is sure he's the one. But when Meri puts her foot in her mouth, things fall apart. Is isn't until the two of them get thrown together working on a book-and-movie project that Jacob realizes his true feelings, and this time he's the one who's starstruck.

China Doll, Barbara Jean Hicks (June 1998)
ISBN 1-57673-262-2
Bronson Bailey is having a mid-life crisis: after years of globetrotting in his journalism career, he's feeling restless. Georgine

Nichols has also reached a turning point: after years of longing for a child, she's decided to adopt. The problem is, now she's fallen in love with Bronson, and he doesn't want a child.

Angel in the Senate, **Kristen Johnson Ingram (April 1998)**
ISBN 1-57673-263-0
Newly elected senator Megan Likely heads to Washington with high hopes for making a difference in government. But accusations of election fraud, two shocking murders, and threats on her life make the Senate take a backseat. She needs to find answers, but she's not sure who she can trust anymore.

Irish Rogue, **Annie Jones**
ISBN 1-57673-189-8
Michael Shaughnessy has paid the price for stealing a pot of gold, and now he's ready to make amends to the people he's hurt. Fiona O'Dea is number one on his list. The problem is, Fiona doesn't want to let Michael near enough to hurt her again. But before she knows it, he's taken his Irish charm and worked his way back into her life…and her heart.

Forgotten, **Lorena McCourtney**
ISBN 1-57673-222-3
A woman wakes up in an Oregon hospital with no memory of who she is. When she's identified as Kat Cavanaugh, she returns to her home in California. As Kat struggles to recover her memory, she meets a fiancé she doesn't trust and an attractive neighbor who can't believe how she's changed. She begins to wonder if she's really Kat Cavanaugh, but if she isn't, what happened to the real Kat?

The Key, **Gayle Roper (April 1998)**
ISBN 1-57673-223-1
On Kristie Matthews's first day living on an Amish farm, she gets bitten by a dog and is rushed to the emergency room by a hand-

some stranger. In the ER, an elderly man in the throes of a heart attack hands her a key and tells her to keep it safe. Suddenly odd accidents begin to happen to her, but no one's giving her any answers.

Tables on the Prairie, Joyce Valdois Smith (May 1998)
ISBN 1-57673-188-X
In the space of a few months, Elise Dumond's life has changed forever. Both her parents are dead, and her family is in danger of losing their farm. Her brother's friend Daniel comes to the rescue and suggests Elise get a job as a Harvey Girl in one of the restaurants "civilizing" the West. The best part for Elise is that she'll get to spend more time with Daniel....

⌒ ANTHOLOGIES ⌒

Fools for Love, Ball, Brooks, Jones
ISBN 1-57673-235-5
By Karen Ball: Kitty starts pet-sitting, but when her clients turn out to be more than she can handle, she enlists help from a handsome handyman.
By Jennifer Brooks: Caleb Murphy tries to acquire a book collection from a widow, but she has one condition: he must marry her granddaughter first.
By Annie Jones: A college professor who has been burned by love vows not to be fooled twice, until her ex-fiancé shows up and ruins her plans!

Heart's Delight, Ball, Hicks, Noble
ISBN 1-57673-220-7
By Karen Ball: Corie receives a Valentine's Day date from her sisters and thinks she's finally found the one...until she learns she went out with the wrong man.
By Barbara Jean Hicks: Carina and Reid are determined to break up their parents' romance, but when it looks like things are

working, they have a change of heart.

By Diane Noble: Two elderly bird-watchers set aside their differences to try to save a park from disaster but learn they've bitten off more than they can chew.

***Snow Swan,* Barbara Jean Hicks** (ISBN 1-57673-107-3)
Toni, an unwed mother and a recovering alcoholic, falls in love
for the first time. But if Clark finds out the truth about her past,
will he still love her?

***Irish Eyes,* Annie Jones** (ISBN 1-57673-108-1)
Julia Reed gets drawn into a crime involving a pot of gold and
has her life turned upside down by Interpol agent Cameron
O'Dea.

***Father by Faith,* Annie Jones** (ISBN 1-57673-117-0)
Nina Jackson buys a dude ranch and hires cowboy Clint Cooper
as her foreman, but her son, Alex, thinks Clint is his new daddy!

***Stardust,* Shari MacDonald** (ISBN 1-57673-109-X)
Gillian Spencer gets her dream assignment but is shocked to
learn she must work with Maxwell Bishop, who once broke her
heart.

***Kingdom Come,* Amanda MacLean** (ISBN 1-57673-120-0)
Ivy Rose Clayborne, M.D., pairs up with the grandson of the coal
baron to fight the mining company that is ravaging her town.

***Dear Silver,* Lorena McCourtney** (ISBN 1-57673-110-3)
When Silver Sinclair receives a letter from Chris Bentley ending
their relationship, she's shocked, since she's never met the man!

***Enough!* Gayle Roper** (ISBN 1-57673-185-5)
When Molly Gregory gets fed up with her three teenaged children, she announces that she's going on strike.

***A Mother's Love,* Bergren, Colson, MacLean**
(ISBN 1-57673-106-5)
Three heartwarming stories share the joy of a mother's love.

Silver Bells, **Bergren, Krause, MacDonald**
(ISBN 1-57673-119-7)
Three novellas focus on romance during Christmastime.

2010

2008

2006

2004

2003
2002

2001

2000